MARY HACKETT:
A SURVEY

Curated by Ann Wilson Lloyd
with contributions by Keith Althaus, Michael Burkard,
Jay Critchley, Jim Peters, Vicky Tomayko
and Rosalind Baker Wilson

PROVINCETOWN ARTS PRESS
INTRODUCTIONS, VOLUME I
Series Editor, Christopher Busa

This catalog was published on the occasion of the exhibition *Mary Hackett: A Survey* at the Cape Museum of Fine Arts, Dennis, Massachusetts, September 22 – November 17, 1996.

Published by Provincetown Arts Press, Inc.
650 Commercial Street, Provincetown, MA 02657

FIRST EDITION

Catalog design: ENS Graphics, Provincetown

Library of Congress Catalog Card Number: 96-70324
ISBN: 0-944854-31-1

PRINTED IN USA

COVER: "Wendy's Room," 1940, oil on board, 20 by 24 inches
Collection of Wendy Everett

BACK COVER: "View of Corn Hill," 1945, oil on board, 20 by 24 inches
Collection of Diana Worthington

C O N T E N T S

	For Mary Hackett	Keith Althaus
5	*Editor's Preface*	Christopher Busa
7	*Curator's Introduction*	Ann Wilson Lloyd
9	*Mary Hackett*	Keith Althaus
33	*Mary Hackett*	Jim Peters Vicky Tomayko
34	*On Mary Hackett: Two Paintings and a Note*	Keith Althaus
37	*Magic Mary Hackett*	Rosalind Baker Wilson
40	*Further Notes on Mary Hackett*	Keith Althaus
42	*"Bubs or Mary": An Interview with Mary Hackett, Provincetown, 1983*	Jay Critchley
46	*Exhibition Checklist*	
	For Mary Hackett	Michael Burkard

Acknowledgements

It has been great fun to organize this survey exhibition of Mary Hackett's work for the Cape Museum of Fine Arts. Her collectors are among the most enthusiastic I have ever worked with. I especially thank her daughter, Wendy Everett, who has been very supportive of both the exhibition and this publication; Keith Althaus and Susan Baker; Christopher Busa, editorial director, and Ewa Nogiec, art director, of the Provincetown Arts Press; Jay Critchley; Jim Peters and Vicky Tomayko; all the lenders to the exhibition and the contributors who funded this publication. Mary might have loved all the fuss, or she might have hated it. Either way, we would have heard about it.

—A.W. L.

This catalog was funded in part by the Massachusetts Cultural Council, a state agency supporting the arts, humanities and sciences which also receives support from the National Endowment for the Arts.

The following individuals and organizations made contributions to the Provincetown Arts Press Mary Hackett Fund:

Anonymous
Adams Pharmacy
Keith Althaus & Susan Baker
Mrs. H. Paul Althaus
William J. Althaus
Gene F. Armstrong
Sally M. Avery
Barbara Baker & Graham Giese
James A. Bayard
Constance J. Black
Eleanor & Ed Bloom
William W. Brill
Alice M. Brock
Peyton Budinger
Jeanne L. Bultman
Michael P. Burkard & Mary Alice Johnston
Cape Air & Nantucket Airlines
Judith Cicero
Georgia M. Coxe
Donald & Nan Brindley Cuba
Elsie Darling
Louise Davy
Blythe & Michael Everett
Tobias Everett & Margot Jackson
Timothy Everett & Lucy Potter
Wendy Everett
Dino & Johanna Fabris
Abby & B.H. Friedman
Miriam Goodman
Linda Graham
Jackson Gregory & Joan Wye
Lee & Patrick Hackett
Tom Hackett
Anna & Philip P. Hamburger
John Hughes & Martha Parker Hall
Noa Hall & Leonora Hall Williams
John Hancock Matching Gift
Ruth Hiebert
Pat Jackson
Denis & Cindy Johnson
Sandra Deer Johnson
Ellen Sinclair Junger
Jon Katz & Paula Span
David Keller & Mary H. Maxwell
A. Thomas Lindsay
Adlin H. Loud
Christopher & Sally Lutz
Bill Maynes Contemporary Art
Hilary Masters
David Lothrop Mayo
Gail B. Mazur
Richard McCann
Heather McHugh & Nikolai Popov
Mary L. Moore
Philip Morris Matching Gift
Ewa Nogiec
Toby & Miriam Olson
Gregory & Trisha Orr
Bill & Cleopatra Mathis Phillips
Germania Phillips
Stephen P. Rand, M.D
Judith Richland & Kevin Shea
Sidney Simon
Heidi Jon Schmidt & Roger Skillings
Jack Shainman Gallery
John Skoyles
Lisa Dawn Sperber
Michael A. Sperber, M.D
Guy Strauss
Joyce & William S. Tager
Mary E. Van Arsdale
Salvador R. Vasques, III
Gloria & Peter Watts
Charles T. & Carol W. Westcott

Editor's Preface

This monograph on Mary Hackett, *Introductions*, Volume I, inaugurates a new series of art publications by the Provincetown Arts Press. Our intention is to introduce significant artists who may be lesser-known, but no less loved, especially because they are original, idiosyncratic, perhaps even self-taught. Less scholarly than the existing *Artists Series*, *Introductions* is offered as an informal *festschrift*, a compilation of various voices striving to articulate something personal in their feeling for the work. In doing so, such authors set a tone, establish a range of reference, and identify the first audience to value the artist's achievement. Thus we introduce Mary Hackett, not as an isolate, but at the center of such attention.

—Christopher Busa
Series Editor

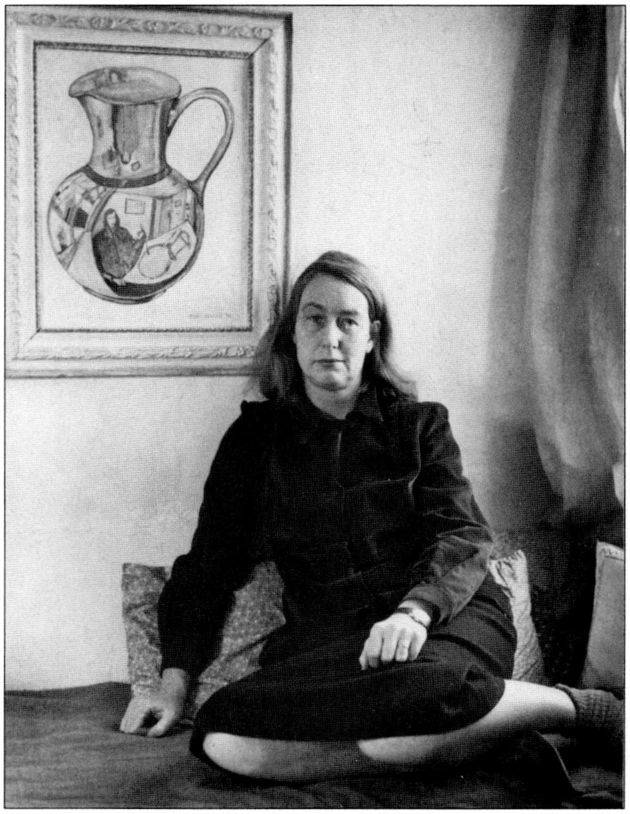

Photo of Mary Hackett by George Yater, c. 1950
Courtesy Shirley Yater and Provincetown Art Association and Museum

Curator's Introduction

I got to meet Mary Hackett, Provincetown's beloved, self-taught painter, during the final months of her life. She had just rejected undergoing an invasive operation for cancer, choosing instead to make the most of her "borrowed time." At 83, in spite of her prognosis and a nearly bedridden physical state, she was ebulliently childlike. She spoke blithely of dying and of planning for certain gifts and legacies to Provincetown (a place she once called the Evil Empire but of late had come to appreciate.) She was, she said, thoroughly enjoying the melodrama of it all—"having fun with death, a subject that's usually kept in the closet."

Mary kept very little in the closet. Along with poignant/amusing takes on world events over the years, she recorded oddly detailed visual narratives of her everyday life. Interiors of her various residences are complete with tangled electrical cords, lampshades askew, notes tacked casually on walls and scattered newspapers with legible headlines of current affairs that concerned her. Her landscapes and street scenes were renderings so visually literal as to include edges of the window frame or car interior where she sat to paint. Ghostly non-sequiturs from a recycled painting might hover absurdly in newer surroundings. From international politics to the quirks of an intense and colorful psyche, Mary Hackett put it all into her work. It was this witty and inventive blend of surprise and frankness that vastly distances her from simple folk artists, or makers of decorative kitsch, whether she was painting on a scrap of two-by-four, on the many metal trays she gave away to friends, or on her favored canvas boards.

Whatever she was like in earlier years, I found Mary Hackett at the end of her life to be as just as brutally honest, as delightfully eccentric, as full of raw charm, as her paintings. It's as if the child in her was never far beneath the surface, that she was perpetually in that rarefied state most artists strive all their lives to regain. Far from being a *naif savant*, Mary was intelligent and sophisticated, worldly and self-aware. "I started to draw for the first time when I was 24," she told me, "and it was as if a child in a mature body was making those drawings. I threw myself back in time and thought, if I had been drawing as a child, this is the way I might have actually done it!" I invite viewers to see her paintings the same way Mary saw her own first drawings—as intuitive, knowing adults endowed with a child's fresh sense of humor, surprise and wonder.

—Ann Wilson Lloyd
Consulting curator of special exhibitions
Cape Museum of Fine Arts

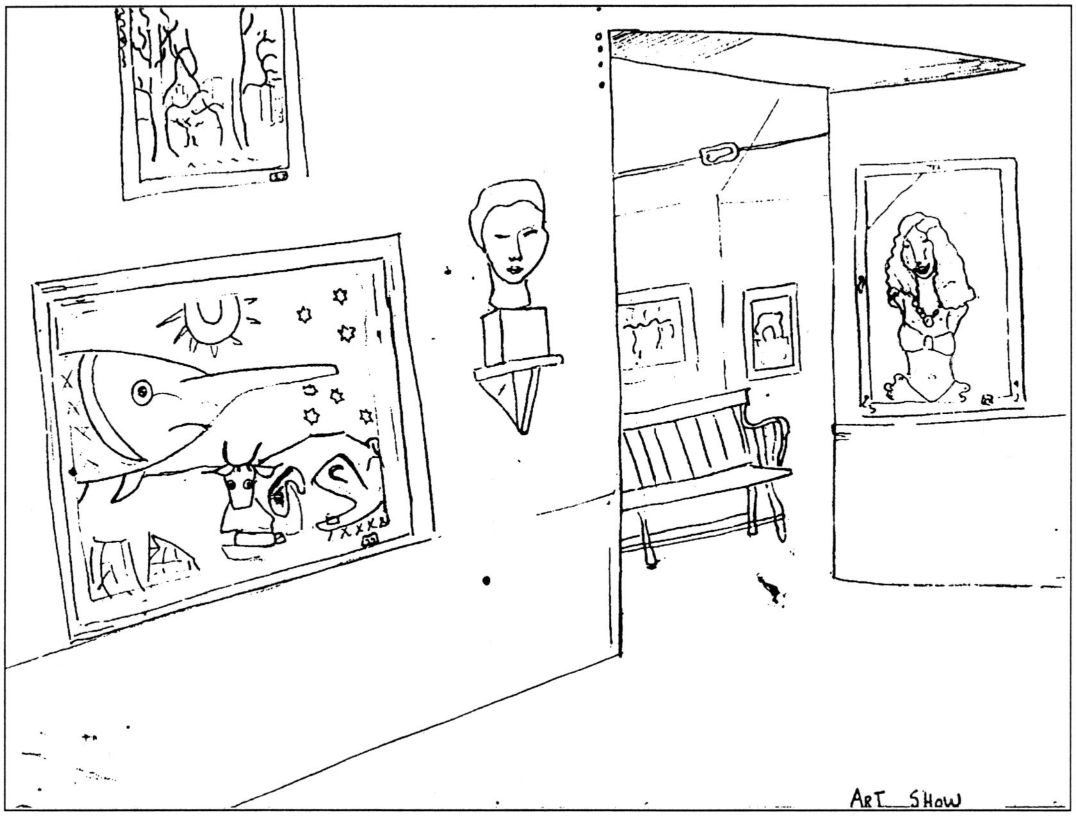

Untitled, pencil on paper, c. 1940s

Mary Hackett

BY KEITH ALTHAUS

"The real thing in art was never reached by professionals, who followed traditional methods of studying and copying, drawing and composition, and who thought of the profit they might earn by their work; it is beyond their ken, because it can be reached only unconsciously by those who have no other intention than to express their own genius or to give vent to the joy and sadness of their hearts."

—Shen Hao, Ch'ing Dynasty painter

It has been said of self-taught artists that they paint not just what they see, but also what they know is there, often defying perspective and other conventions to tell us what they know and want to impart, not unlike map-makers who must distort in order to be truthful.

Mary Hackett was a self-taught artist and this dictum may apply to her on a literal basis in a few cases, but in a metaphoric sense it applies to all her work. She knew more than the picture could tell us and repeatedly told what she knew, not through keys or clues, for they are in the old language of symbolism, but in the unconscious detail, and unspoken strangeness, unsought and completely natural, which charge her work with the vividness of what's there and the surprise of what's not. Like few others her paintings are truly magnetic.

With its tradition of individualism and independence, America has created a constant stream of iconoclast artists. In a country synonymous with change, it is not surprising that over time a positive "tradition of the new" took root, overtaking all other, more traditional forms, to become, and remain, the art of our time. Even within such freedom, schools and movements developed, and others remained outside them. Such artists tend to leave admirers rather than followers. With them it is often their fellow artists who are their earliest and most ardent supporters. The Cornells, the Ryders, the Eilshemiuses, the Neels, must always coexist in our consciousness with the prevailing trends, and fight for recognition in a roomful of talents who draw attention to, and include by reference, each other. These loners are liable to be forgotten. We remember the movements, their leaders, and gradually we recall the followers, but we are still likely to forget the outsider, whose is always a lone voice.

If not discouraged by such obscurity and lack of recognition, there can be benefits to an artist: a career whose trajectory is unaffected by the gravitational pull of the marketplace, or the proximity of criticism, which can lead to self-consciousness, or over-intellectualized efforts to meet or surpass the critic's expectations. Another benefit can be a surprising variety and adventurousness, often curbed by the invisible presence of the market and the critic. Few choose this path. It is fortunate Mary Hackett was not so deterred or intimidated. Her life's work is a monument of single-mindedness and disregard for convention. Whatever price she may have paid, she left us a legacy of beauty, strangeness, humor, and mystery.

I

The earliest works we have of Mary Hackett's are drawings from 1932. She was then 26 years old. Her drawings from the start exhibited an assurance and strength of line that are surprising in a beginning artist. She continued drawing for several years before she took up painting. Two things are striking about this: from the beginning she made a decision not to seek any formal training. Art lessons would have been the logical step for someone in her position. This decision confirms the confidence and assurance apparent in the drawing. Also it implies she saw, even at this early stage, that there was something in her work so unique and valuable, that it outweighed the obvious advantages of formal training and instruction. Throughout her life she was aware of various holes in her talent: on the back of one painting she writes that the nose is uncomplimentary but only because "she can't do noses." This was a small sacrifice to one so intent upon retaining her own uniqueness, and so fearful of influences. It is ironic that she, who felt herself so extremely suggestible, went on to create such an inimitable body of work. We also should remember this was before there was much interest in American "primitive" painting or so-called "folk" artists; no thought was given to appealing to an existing audience, or fitting into a recognizable school. One advantage to having started late was that she was unencumbered by years of exposure to criticism and rhetoric, which could limit the artist, locking her in to tried and acceptable paths. Instead she experienced the great freedom of discovering a broad new expanse which she could explore without a lot of restricting rules reverberating in her head. Such determination and independence is rare in anyone, let alone a young woman of that time. Though adventurous and open in other aspects of her life, she was perhaps trying to conserve an original, a first vision, which once altered or lost cannot quickly be recovered. Like the writer afraid of discussing a work-in-progress, knowing how easily it is squandered and diluted in conversation, so perhaps she sensed the fragility of creative intensity, how reliant it is upon secrecy and silence. Today it is hard to imagine any course of instruction, or method of teaching, that would have left her singular talent intact, or left us so unique a body of work. Thus the decision made by the young wife today seems almost prescient.

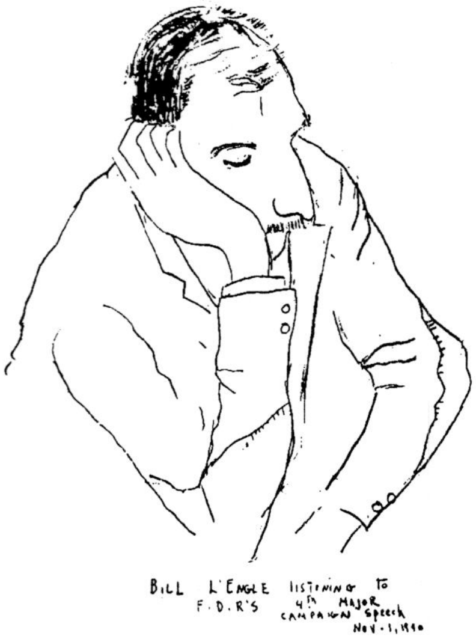

Bill L'Engle Listening to F.D.R.'s 4th Major Campaign Speech, Nov. 1, 1940
Pencil on paper

A second striking quality of her drawings is the difficult subject matter she often chose. Throughout her life, technically challenging vantage points and daunting prospects attracted her, as well as the most complex and demanding subjects. That she chose to make drawings of ships' riggings and automobile engines, shows not only rare patience and lack of interest in the product as marketable, but perhaps also a mind invoking order, seeking a necessary equilibrium between complexity and simplicity, even as we balance the vastness and ingenuity of our brains with the blunt desires of our hearts, running the gamut between Piranesian intricacy and an emotional monotone. Even in the complicated drawings, a great simplicity comes forth; when erasures are evident there is nothing tentative about the line. Her subjects imply an unexpected faith in the viewer, to be not only interested in, but able to follow probably unfamiliar mechanisms and gears. These drawings laid the groundwork for the single object paintings of chairs, clocks, and typewriters, which in turn echo the lessons of strength of line, sureness of vision, and a certain fearlessness, which at once excludes the viewer as pre-critic, inhibitor, and includes him as a worthy and intelligent audience. Skills developed wrestling with these difficult subjects contributed to the "simpler" work to follow. These paintings of spare and unadorned objects are heirs of the ability to see, learned from this precocious beginning. Their complexity is buried, layered and psychological rather than obvious and visible, and thus all the more effective and haunting.

II

So strong a beginning, and one to which she devoted so much time before starting to paint, laid the groundwork for a painting style in which drawing was a more than equal component with coloring and composition and surface treatment. This reliance on drawing within the paintings bears comparison with the paintings of the ancient Greeks. In her earliest paintings the paint is heavier and there is less drawing, or the line is thicker, but the subjects and composition are already recognizably hers. Drawing for her was largely a matter of the line in space; shading and volume were elements reserved for her painting. Her experience of the blankness of the paper translated into the special quality of the space in her paintings. She had the confidence to use empty space in bold and quirky ways. Sometimes the space is disconcerting and unsettling, just as silence can be. Our natural tendency seems to be to fill in, to cover, the exposed silence or space. It is a nervousness that can be overcome. But looking at pictures is by nature meditative, and eventually we quiet to a state receptive to the new or unfamiliar. Her own dismissal of the superfluous, and her embrace of the spare and the unadorned, resulted in pictures that are subtly provocative. She is close to the self-taught artists mentioned above, in that she did not "doctor" the paintings to make them more readable or familiar, she did not fill in the gaps for the sake of convention. Her faithfulness to her subjects was untroubled by a need to please.

Perhaps the clearer success of her early drawings, and their mastery of challenging material, compared with the cruder attempts of her first paintings, led her to incorporate more drawing into them. Perhaps the seductive nature of the line simply surfaced in the paintings without forethought or planning—whatever, by the mid and late '30s, her drawing-in-painting was well established, and would be her dominant style for the remainder of her life. The bold, but coarse line of some of the early paintings became the refined and subtle definition of the later works. Even at its heaviest her line is never gross or plodding, the thick-as-headlines, blunt instrument of missionary realism, leaving subjects placard-stiff, and confining them to a single destiny. Nor at its lightest does it bear comparison with the illustration of the day, which hints at and alludes to things more ideal than real, behind the ephemeral veil of technique. Hers was an inner darkness, and an inner light. And both were faithful to her, throughout her life, alternating like the beacon of a lighthouse.

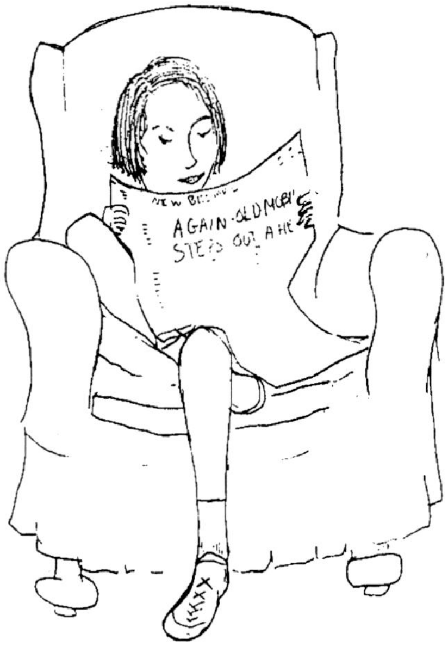

Untitled, pencil on paper

Drawing led to painting, and the painting incorporated the drawing, and she continued with both her entire career. Her output was never very great, in the course of five decades she perhaps created 300 canvases or less. Compared with many others that is not terribly productive. Most artists, however, are men, who, are often ruthless in their efforts to divest themselves of obligations except those of their art. The artist who is a wife and mother is rarely able to be so free. Mary Hackett certainly tried, but the domesticity of much of her subject matter, its closeness to home, shows how hard it was to escape these ties. The positive result is the great intimacy of her interiors, her most singular contribution.

III

In a small body of work, Mary Hackett produced an amazing variety. There are her landscapes, which include true landscapes, of mountains, rivers, scenes around the Cape, as well as those centered upon architecture, both great and small, from Notre Dame to a bandstand in Oaxaca, from cathedrals to a frozen custard stand. Her portraits extend from her family and friends to some known only from afar such as John Lennon, and her great favorite Abraham Lincoln There are her interiors, ranging from her living room, her kitchen, rooms where she is staying, to large, public interiors, of museums, churches, a garage, a gallery. Her paintings of single objects differ in feeling from still lifes and in some way are closer to portraits. The object enlarged as to take up almost the whole canvas, or set floating in space with no background, can take on a specter-like or apparitional quality. We view them very differently from the same objects set in their usual background. Like the silvery white backdrop the photographer uses to isolate and bring forward the subject, Hackett isolated subjects compel us to see the object without references. A clock spinning with the mystery of time or a typewriter carrying the enigma of language are hardly simple objects. But nothing about Mary Hackett was simple.

The word "magic" has been applied to her work many times. Her daughter Wendy Everett recalls her using it to describe both her initial discovery of painting and her subsequent experiences with it. When we call something charming we are usually far from recalling the sense of charm, as a spell, or an object that has a hold over us which is not readily explainable. But that is just the sense in which it applies to Hackett. There is certainly no sleight-of-hand in these paintings, if anything they disarm us with their simplicity and directness. They often seem to greet us, as if we were expected. The door has been left open. Although we often find ourselves looking through windows and doors in her work, nothing is voyeuristic. Often they seem to "frame" another picture, within the larger painting, even as she often includes paintings on the walls. These interiors are invitations: to sit at her desk, read her unfinished letters, see the books she's reading, to notice the coats hanging on their pegs, the unmade bed, the dishes in the sink. They are extraordinarily intimate, unusual both for their time and for their apparent casualness. Certain paintings are also magical because they invoke a field of influence, which although we cannot actually explain its power over us, affects us, much as ritual objects or the cave paintings of an early people might, though we do not subscribe to their belief system.

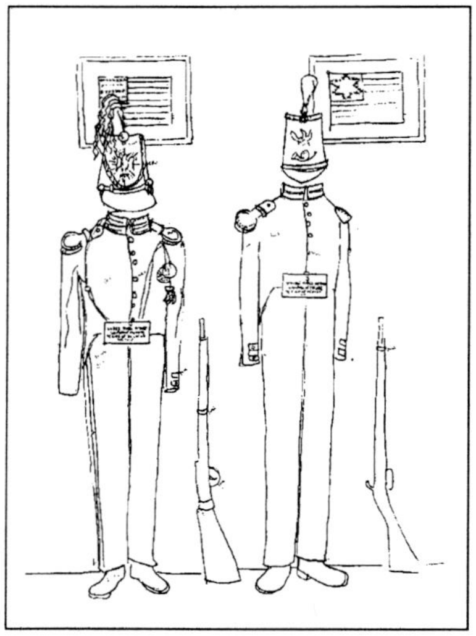

Civil War Uniforms (Smithsonian)
Pencil on paper

One reason her work, even her lesser pieces, holds our interest, is because none of them, except those deliberately humorous (and play was important to her), was undertaken frivolously. Each represents an occasion she was moved to paint. In this she differs greatly from the studio painters who experiment every day in hope of discovering something which will stimulate them further. Problems developed in her work which had to be solved, but never were the works primarily acts of problem solving. And although a seeker all her life, she was not searching for something with which to impress us. And none of her paintings comes across to us as a mere exercise. As very often with the visionary artist, the painting is already realized before she starts to paint, and the task is to faithfully execute it. Mary Hackett was often far harsher than we would be in her assessments written on the backs of her paintings, because she retained some vision of what they might have been. Though in some the spell is weaker than in others, we are always aware of it. And once an object is imbued with magic it never wears off.

Mary Hackett's talent was not to make the ordinary beautiful, or interesting, or even strange, but through intense concentration, and purity of will, to lift it, beyond, into a realm where we can see that these were real moments, real places and people, in a life like our own, which is not boring and mean, but which is valuable, if only we can remember it. Her paintings are mnemonic devices for remembering life.

IV

Why her paintings seem so fresh to us today is partly a function of their true value and partly an accident. So many features of her work for 50 years—the incorporation of writing or "text" in the paintings; her sometime hallucinatory scenes, as when Lincoln appears in her living room; the intimate, unstaged atmosphere of her interiors; her wit and playfulness—strike us as thoroughly contemporary. But the real modernity in her work lies in its uncanny psychological content. Everything from her single objects, in their "objectness," to her self-portrait with eyes closed, to the telling details of her interiors, impart a far more knowing aspect than many planned and plotted paintings. Because she did not follow the current of the times, her work has not dated. And because she did not censor out the unpretty in favor of the pretty, leaving as she did the clutter, the electrical wires and sockets, the unmade bed and dirty dishes, we are not surprised to find John Lennon or a TV set appearing in her pictures. That she is viewing on TV both world events, like Nixon's inauguration or an addictive soap opera, seems entirely appropriate. Though she disliked clutter she painted it because it was challenging, or as she said, "What would be interesting about a made bed?" Having made no effort to "fit in" early, later there were none of those unseemly efforts to seem relevant that can mar the ends of careers.

The frank lack of pretense, in herself and her work, made her a favorite of a new generation in her later years in Provincetown. Many of the established artists seemed complacent and scripted compared to her adventurousness, and their works related to the past rather than the present. How did she react to the artistic community in which she lived? One clue perhaps is contained in the wonderful, "Looking Down Nickerson Street," painted from in front of her house, facing the bay. In the right-hand side of the picture there is the hunched-over figure of Hans Hofmann putting out his trash. As in much Asian art the figure is set within the landscape, going about his business, not dominating it. The ordinariness which was worthy of recording in her own life was equally true for others. She had only one standard. That art for her was an activity not separate from other human activities is exemplified by various touches she gave her home, from little signs and reminders, to paintings on the furniture and floors.

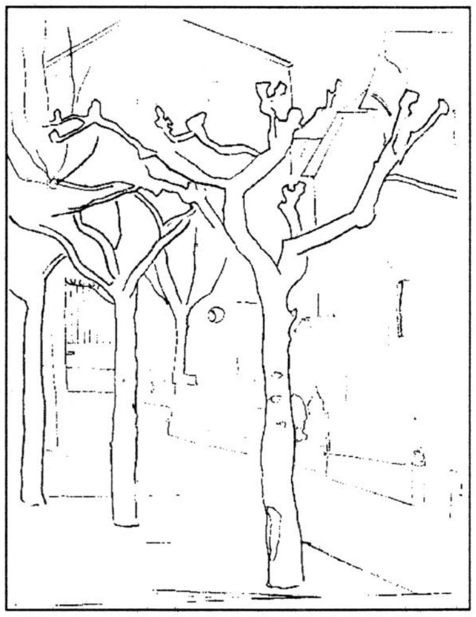

Pollarded Trees
Pencil on paper

How did she handle her own lack of recognition? She could not have painted the wise and beautiful paintings she did and not have been aware of her genius. Nor could she be unaware of the success of much of the mediocrity around her. She did not have to bear the full burden of this lack of recognition as one who is a "full-time" artist might, the dual roles of mother and housewife deflected some of its impact. Her confidence in her work is borne out by the fact she kept at it faithfully for over 50 years. Some of her contemporaries betray an insecurity in their ever-changing modes and styles, disguised as exploration. There are always those who will understand and a word from them can be worth more than ceaseless praise from the wrong quarters. Still the dichotomy between knowing one's own worth inwardly and being so undervalued in the world must have had its effect on her. In her case I think she occasionally feigned an almost dismissive attitude toward her work, sometimes treating cavalierly the canvases stacked in her upstairs studio. Yet at the same time she was extremely protective of them, and careful to see it did not fall into the "wrong hands." That she was not reliant upon the sale of paintings for income can also not be underestimated as a liberating factor, allowing her both to create the time to paint, and then to extend a kind of stewardship over her work. We are the beneficiaries of both.

V

Everyone familiar with Mary Hackett's work has noted at one time or another the writing she did on the backs of her paintings. Text in the form of signs, advertising, titles, etc., was always important to her. But the writing on the back has a special place in her work. She often titled and dated her paintings on the back, sometimes she added information such as directions(along with a snapshot) of how to get to the site of the painting, a newspaper photograph that inspired the painting, and various asides about the work. In 1973 she apparently went through all the paintings in her possession and wrote in a large hand, using black paint, commentary on each of the paintings. This ranges from simple identification and dating to her opinion. Like the earlier mention of her trouble painting noses, she can be self-deprecating:

> The Hudson at Nyack 1952
> "Those white objects are supposed to be ice."

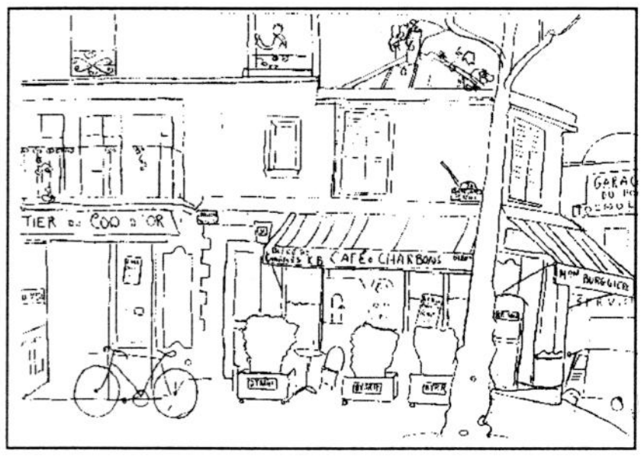

Paris Street Scene
Pencil on paper

On a painting in which a small dog appears in a corner of a couch, she can be personal and retrospective;

> "I cherish this rare reproduction of beloved dog Muffy Chargo—
> I still dream about him regularly"

And she can be informative:

> "View from interior of Peugeot auto in Paris looking out at the Seine
> 1961. M.H. in process of trying to paint a saint rather than the scene."

which helps us understand what the artist, unseen but for brush and canvas in the foreground, and her eyes reflected in the rearview mirror, is trying to do. They can be insightful, wry, and poignant all in the space of a few lines. And they are an invaluable addition to our understanding. They show her working within a third dimension, Time. Telling us about the past and present of the painting. For instance, "Self-portrait: Dying at Eighteen," "Done over an unsatisfactory portrait of Dorothy Day," shows us that for her what has been painted out is still part of the painting, and she wants us to know it also. It is not planned like Rauschenberg's "Erased DeKooning," yet the information becomes part of our understanding of the painting in a similar way. The strange and unique illustrations of *The Hound of Heaven* by Francis Thompson, which she completed at the end of her life, similarly owe something to the photographs in a paperback edition of the poem over which she painted, although nearly completely obliterated by the painting she credited them with inspiring her. She could continue to work on paintings left unfinished long before, or on ones she considered failures. Drawing over them, adding photographs, cutout pictures, pasting on objects. As long as they were in her possession they were salvageable.

VI

As with any artist, no matter how much information we uncover, there will always be areas of dispute and or uncertainty. A hundred questions must go unanswered. An artist of as many facets and as much variety as Hackett will draw admirers to all her stages and aspects. And likely appreciating one aspect will lead to an appreciation of another. Many are first drawn to her for her quirkiness and what is seen as eccentricity, at least for its time. Later they will discover that independent and unconventional approach put to deeper purposes. Interestingly, among her friends she was not alone. With boldness and innovation. Edmund Wilson established himself outside of academia as America's pre-eminent man of letters, and Dorothy Day, also working outside conventional roles, spirited the Catholic Worker movement. Some of that generation which came of age before the Depression continued to apply models of liberation and independence acquired in the '20s to those deadening and increasingly conformist times.

It is the hubris of every age, that it will not commit the oversights and slights of the previous era. The rejection of the Impressionists, the Fauves, etc., seems inconceivable to us today. Then it was serious business. Laboring without recognition is all the harder for each age's pretense to objectivity and omniscience. I am reminded of the title of Dorothy Day's autobiography, *The Long Loneliness*, lying in clear view in one of Mary Hackett's late interiors. Amid all the exuberance and joy of her work which is so winning, I often return to a curious and minor work, done on a board, from a broken piece of furniture, curved and stained, which she painted over: on one side there is a pale hand in the center of a dark rectangle, everything surrounding it is murky, there are no other clear images. It is called, "Help." It was painted from a newspaper photo of a hand seen in a window of a burning building engulfed in smoke. The board's other side is taken up by two profiles of the same old-fashioned brass key, on one there is a small red stain, and in the corner of the painting in fine print is written: "No matter how well I polish the key on one side the blood stain only disappears to reappear on the other, as in Blue Beard." Sometimes looking at these unhappy images, so silent and cold, far from the joyous horse kicking up its heels, the wry and witty portraits, the enchanting interiors, I feel the clear, unflinching gaze of the painter. And equally sometimes, drawn to some small detail, lovingly and tenderly rendered: flowers on a desk, a painting within a painting, hung crookedly over a mantle, it is hard to suppress a smile, or feel less than an exhilaration and pure happiness, one almost unattached to the subject, a free-floating joy. The contradictions and complexity of such a artist make us continually dive deeper, and we are continually rewarded.

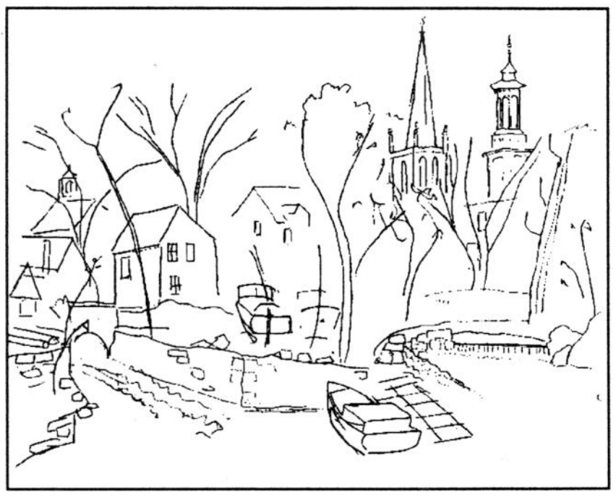

Untitled, pencil on paper

VII

Comparison and commentary can be meaningless. Alone with a painting, away from all the writing and talk, reputation and expectation, away, if we will let ourselves, from our own preconceptions, about skill and the lack thereof, about message and beauty, simply alone with the canvas certain things will either shine through, or their absence will be apparent. Coleridge long ago defined the difference between what he called Imagination and what he called Fancy. The two are continually confused; time however does have a way of sorting them out. Fancy comes from the top of the head, no necessity drives it, it grows in very shallow soil. Imagination has deep roots, can never be mistaken for mere cleverness. Its mystery, which we may never unravel, goes round and round, its energy is inexhaustible. We are constantly being fooled, misled, led down blind alleys, only to retrace our steps, guided not by an unerring instinct for the true, but a disillusion with the false. Every wrong step in the maze adds to our knowledge. Whatever we tire of is a burden lifted from us; we can approach what we've overlooked from the beginning, as obvious, spurned for its simplicity. Allied with no school, or system of ideas, but simply following her heart, Mary Hackett has had to wait to find her audience.

Keith Althaus is the author of a volume of poems, Rival Heavens, *published by the Provincetown Arts Press.*

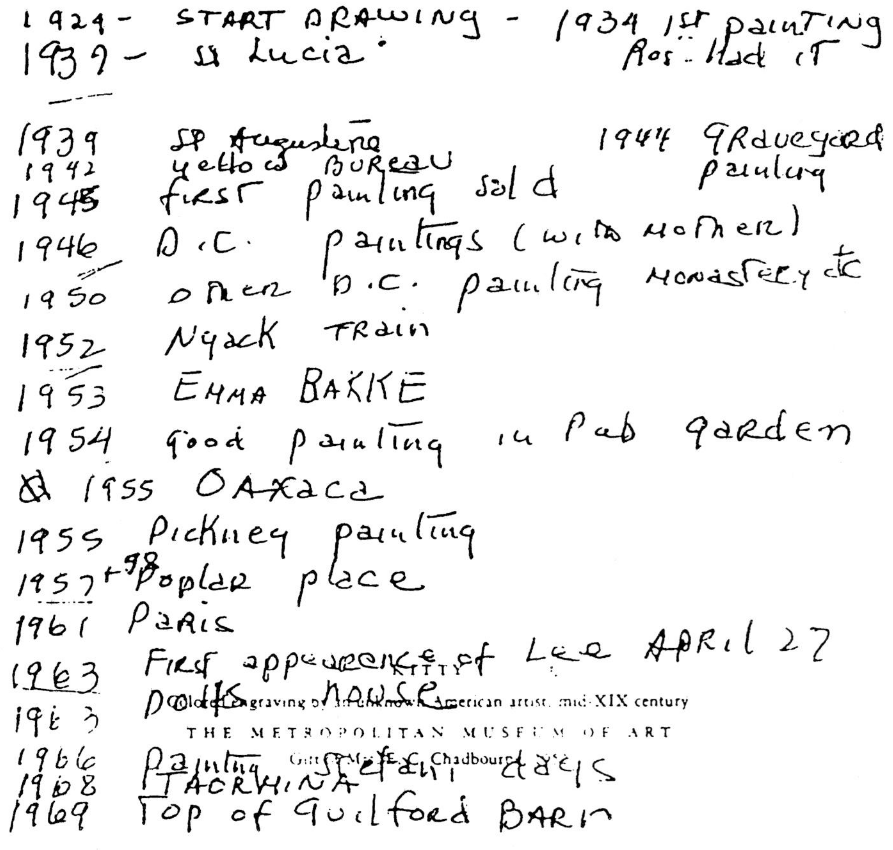
1924 - START DRAWING - 1934 1st painting
1939 - St Lucia · Ros. had it

1939 St Augustine 1944 graveyard painting
1942 yellow Bureau
1945 first painting sold
1946 D.C. paintings (with mother)
1950 other D.C. painting monastery etc
1952 Nyack Train
1953 EMMA BAKKE
1954 good painting in Pub garden
1955 OAXACA
1955 Pickney painting
1957+58 Poplar place
1961 Paris
1963 First appearance of Lee APRIL 27
1963 dolls house
1966 painting Stefani dates
1968 TACRHINA
1969 Top of Guilford Barn

KITTY
Colored engraving by an unknown American artist, mid-XIX century
THE METROPOLITAN MUSEUM OF ART
Chadbourne

Mary Hackett, Personal Chronology, 1969

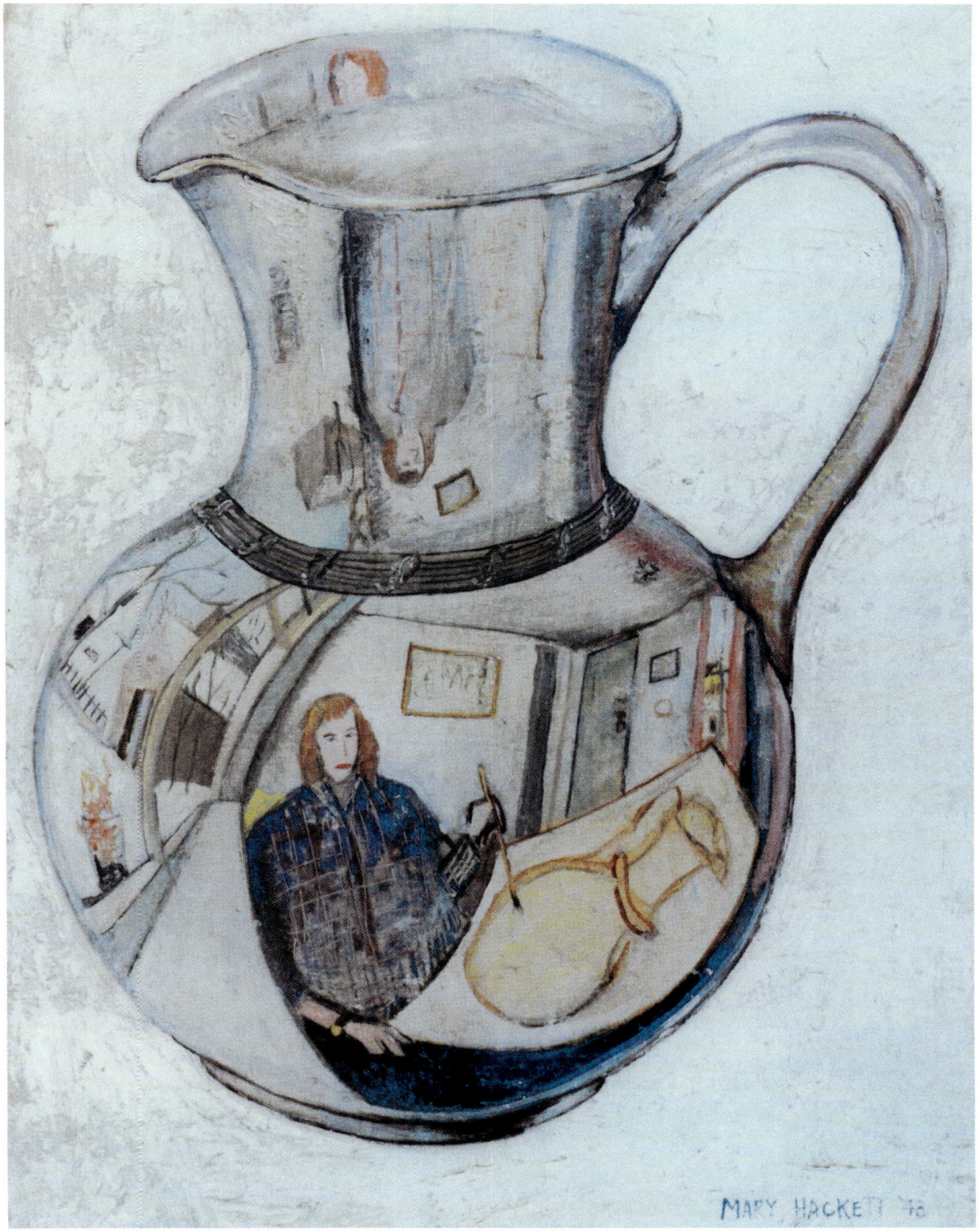

The Silver Pitcher, 1948
Oil on canvas board, 20 by 16 inches
Collection of Wendy Everett

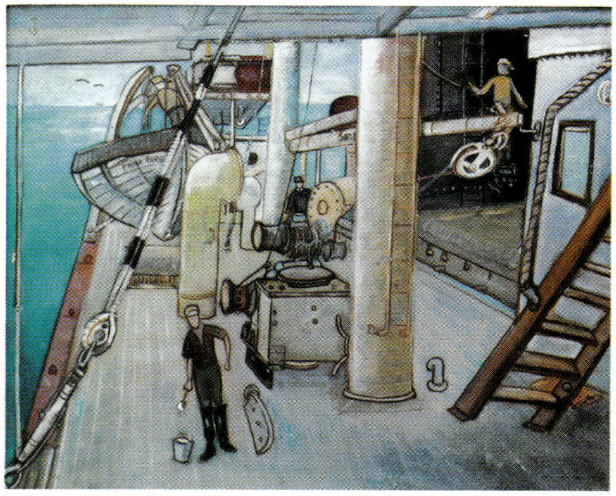

Deck of the Emma Bakke, 1953
Oil on canvas board, 16 by 20 inches
Collection of Susan Baker

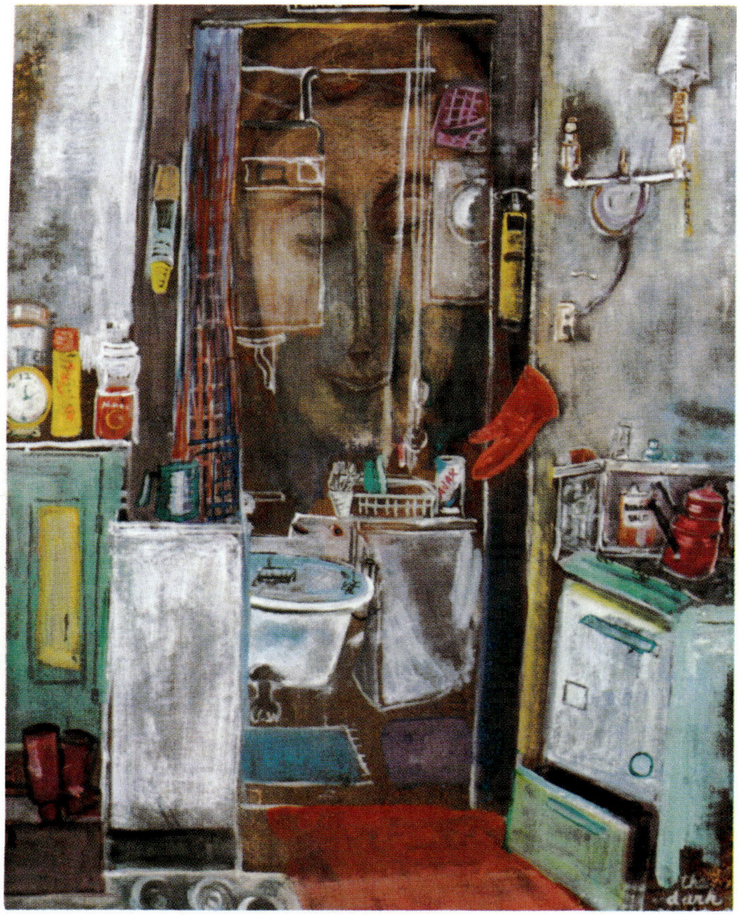

Dark Night of Clutter, (dated 1923) c.1930s
Oil on board, 20 by 16 inches
Collection of Ellery Althaus

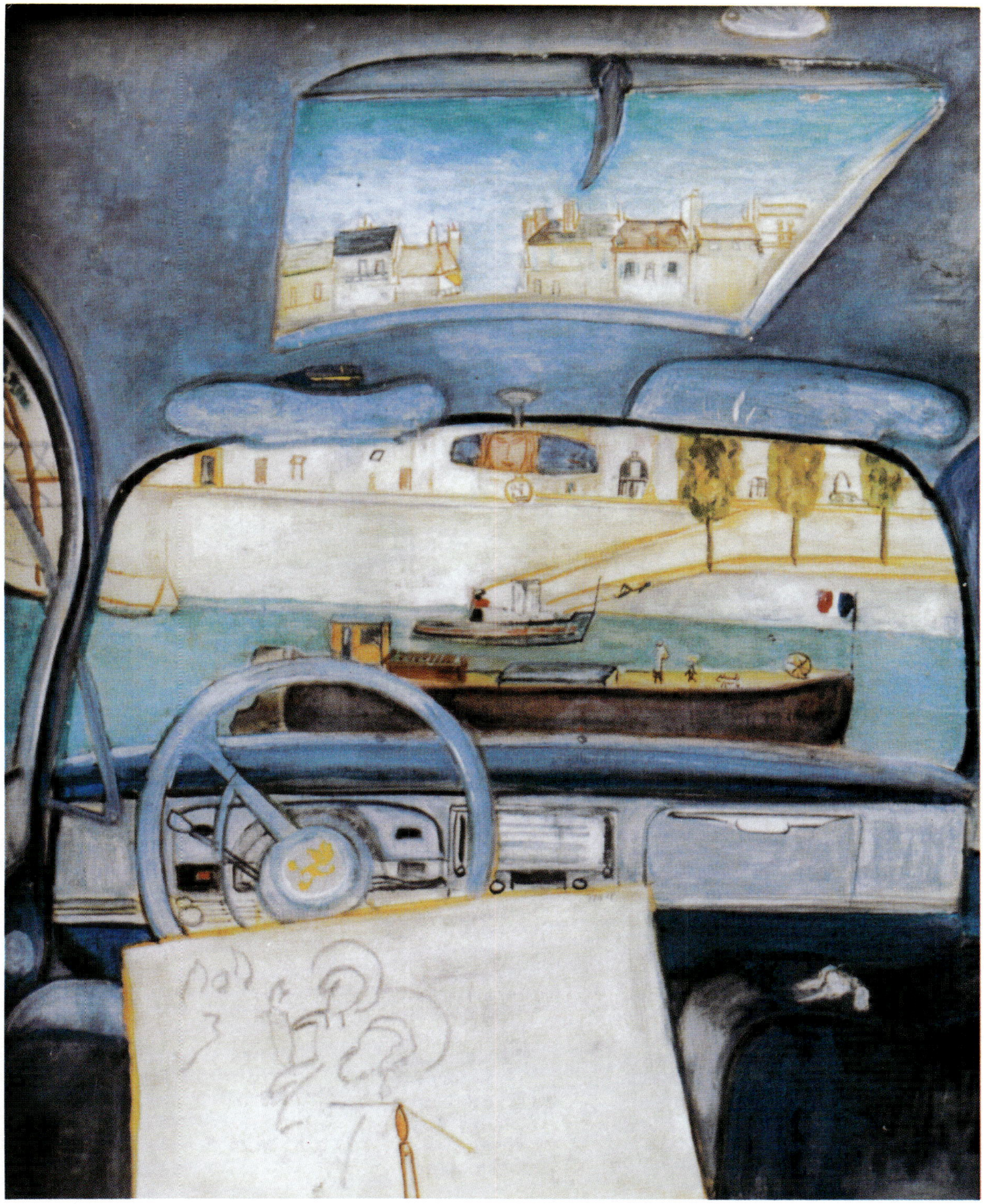

View from Peugeot, Paris, 1961
Oil on wood, 20 by 16 inches
Collection of Susan Baker

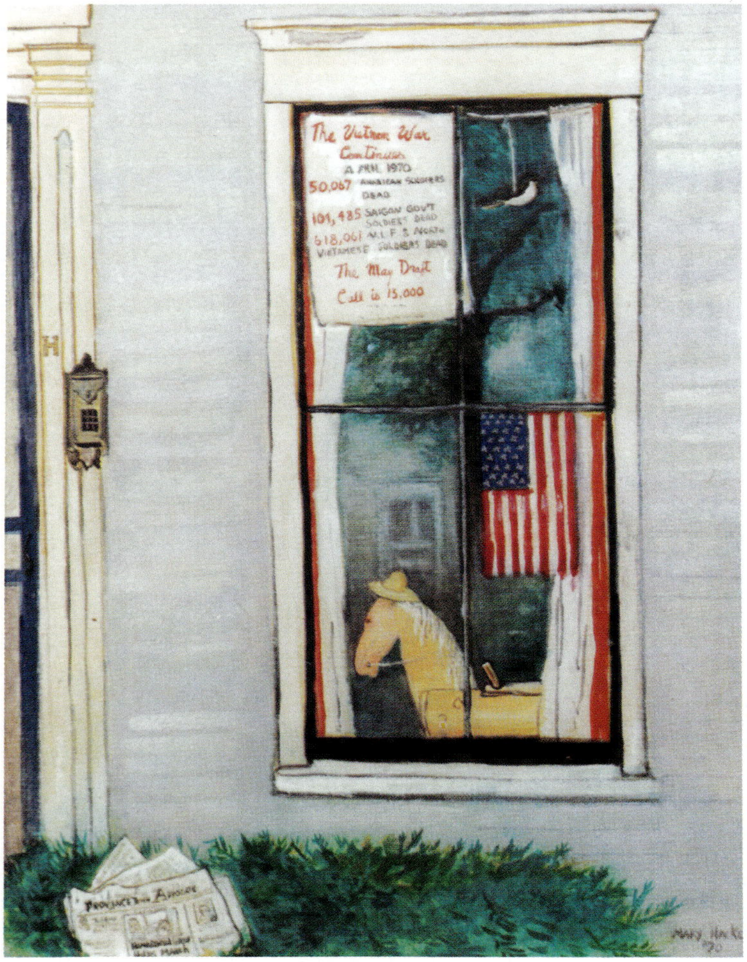

The Vietnam War, 1970
Oil on canvas board, 20 by 16 inches
Collection of Frank Schaefer

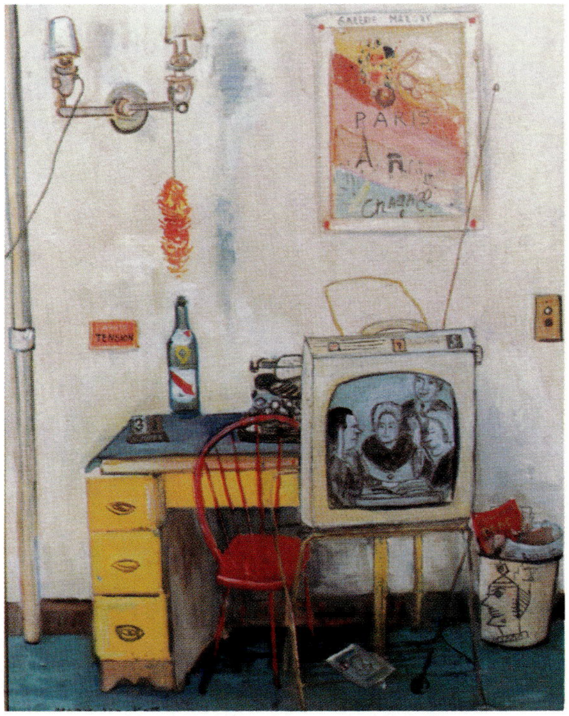

Nixon Taking Oath of Office, January 20, 1973, 1960, 1973
Oil on canvas board, 20 x 16 inches
Private Collection

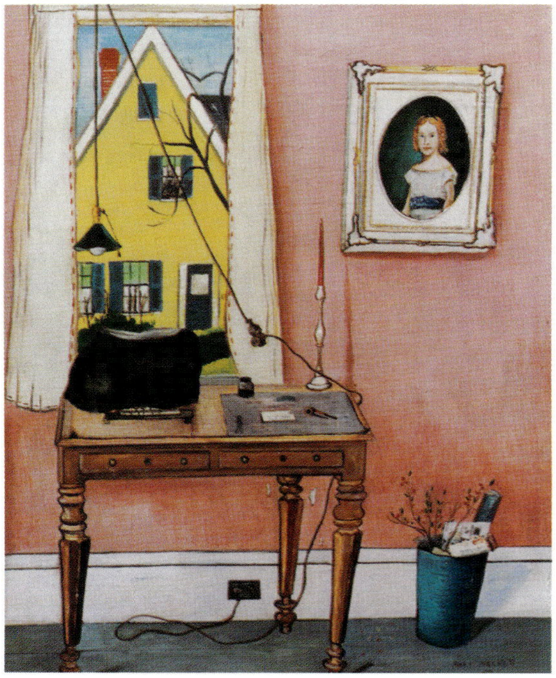

The Front Room, 1947
Oil on canvas board, 20 by 24 inches
Collection of John Dowd

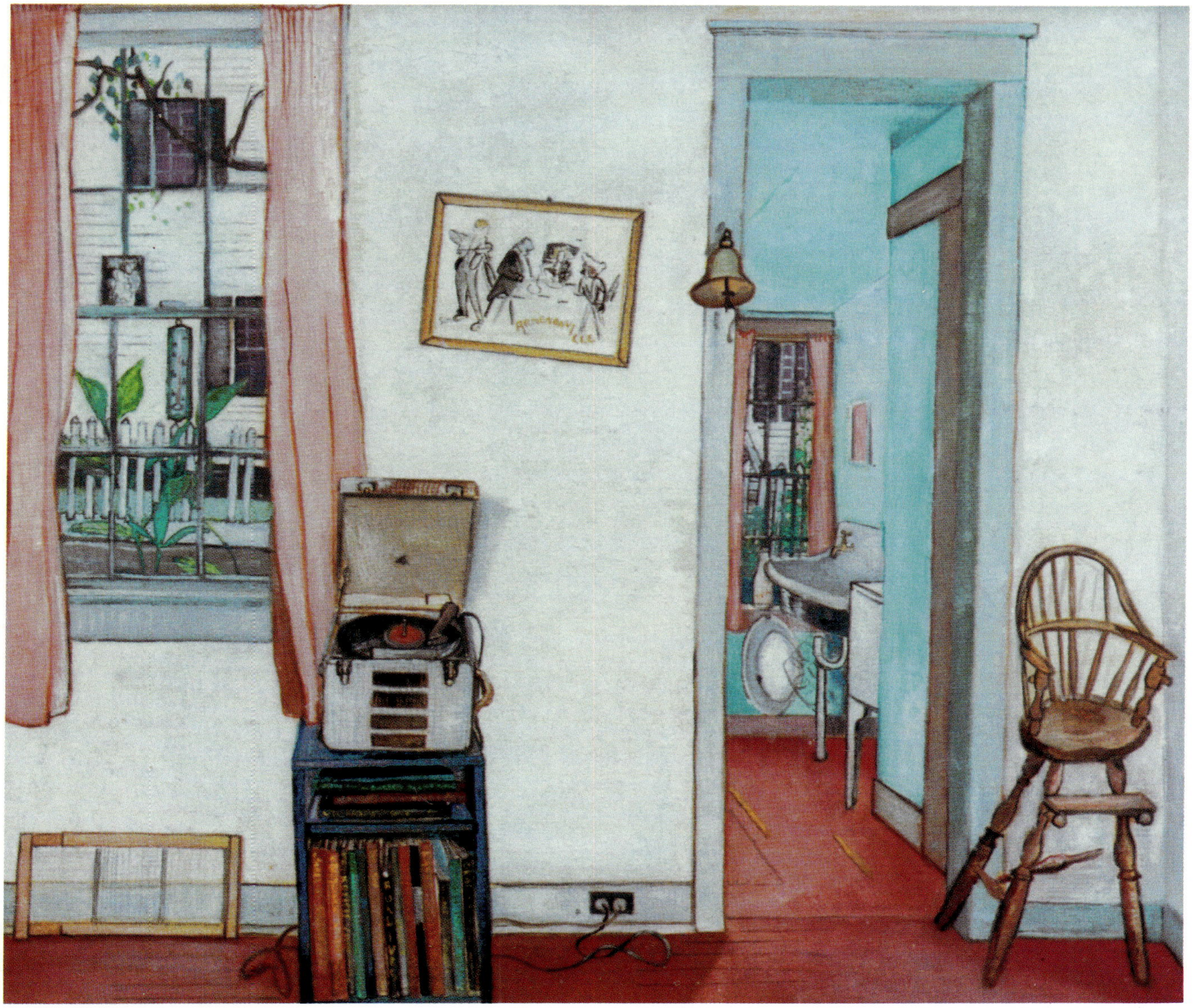

Untitled (Nickerson Street Interior), c. 1950s
Oil on canvas board, 20 by 24 inches
Collection of Miriam Goodman

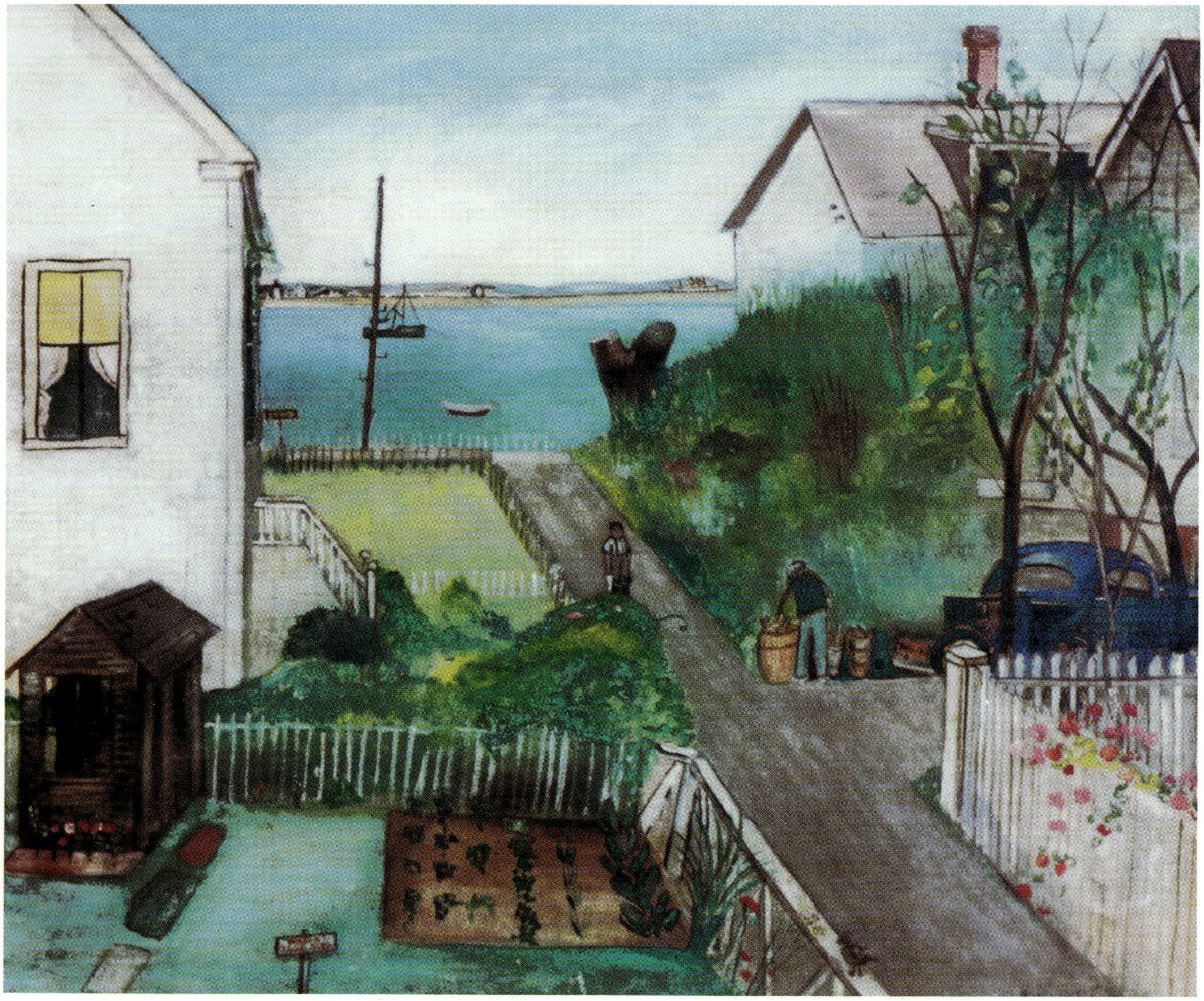

View Down Nickerson Street of Hans Hofmann Emptying His Trash, 1946
Oil on canvas board, 20 by 24 inches
Collection of Wendy Everett

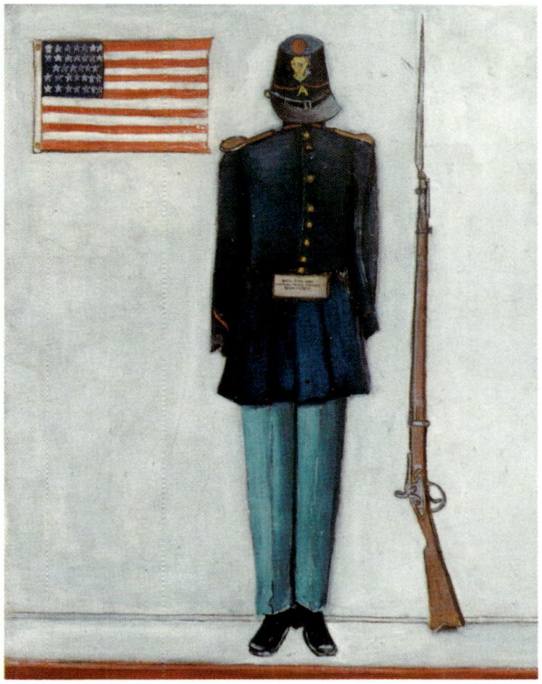

Untitled (Civil War Uniform from the Smithsonian), c. 1930s
Oil on canvas board, 20 by 16 inches
Collection of Anna and Philip Hamburger

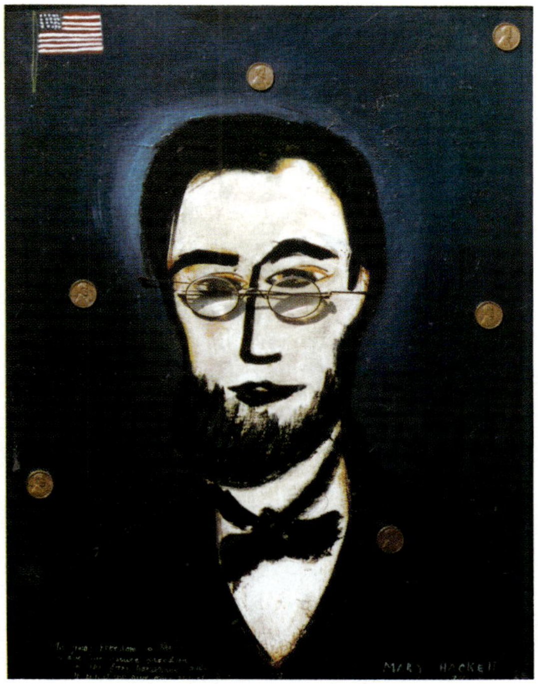

Abraham Lincoln, 1973
Oil on canvas board, mixed media, 20 by 16 inches
Collection of John Dowd

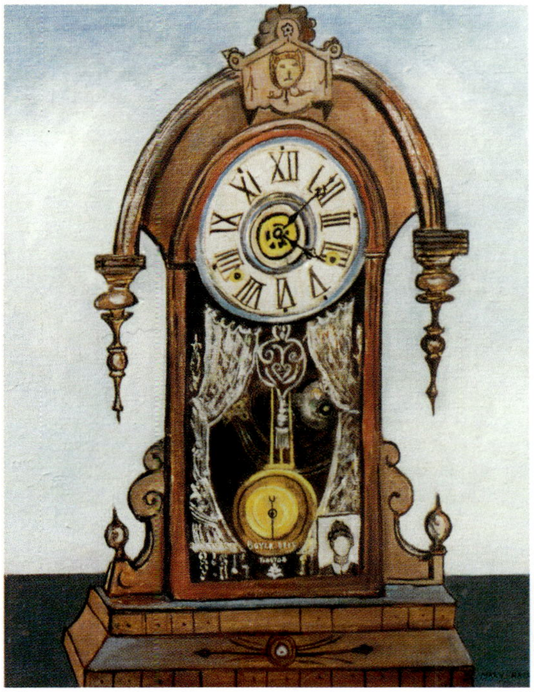

Guilford Clock, n.d.
Oil on canvas board, 20 by 16 inches
Collection of John Dowd

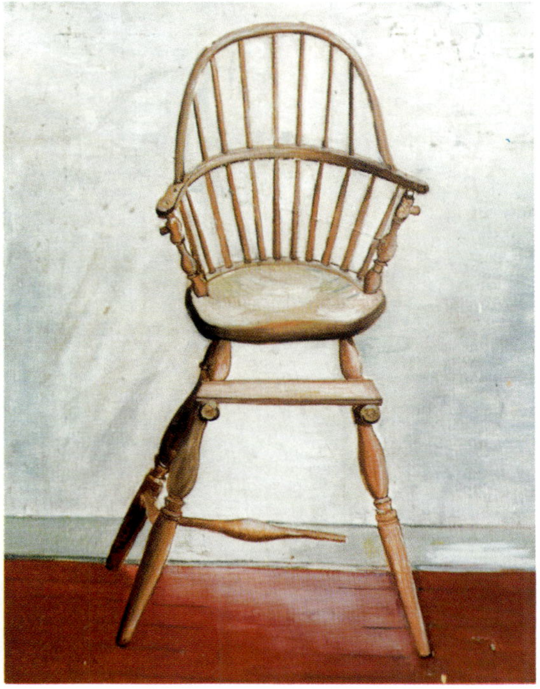

Coulton's Baby Chair, 1946
Oil on canvas board, 20 by 16 inches
Collection of Anna and Philip Hamburger

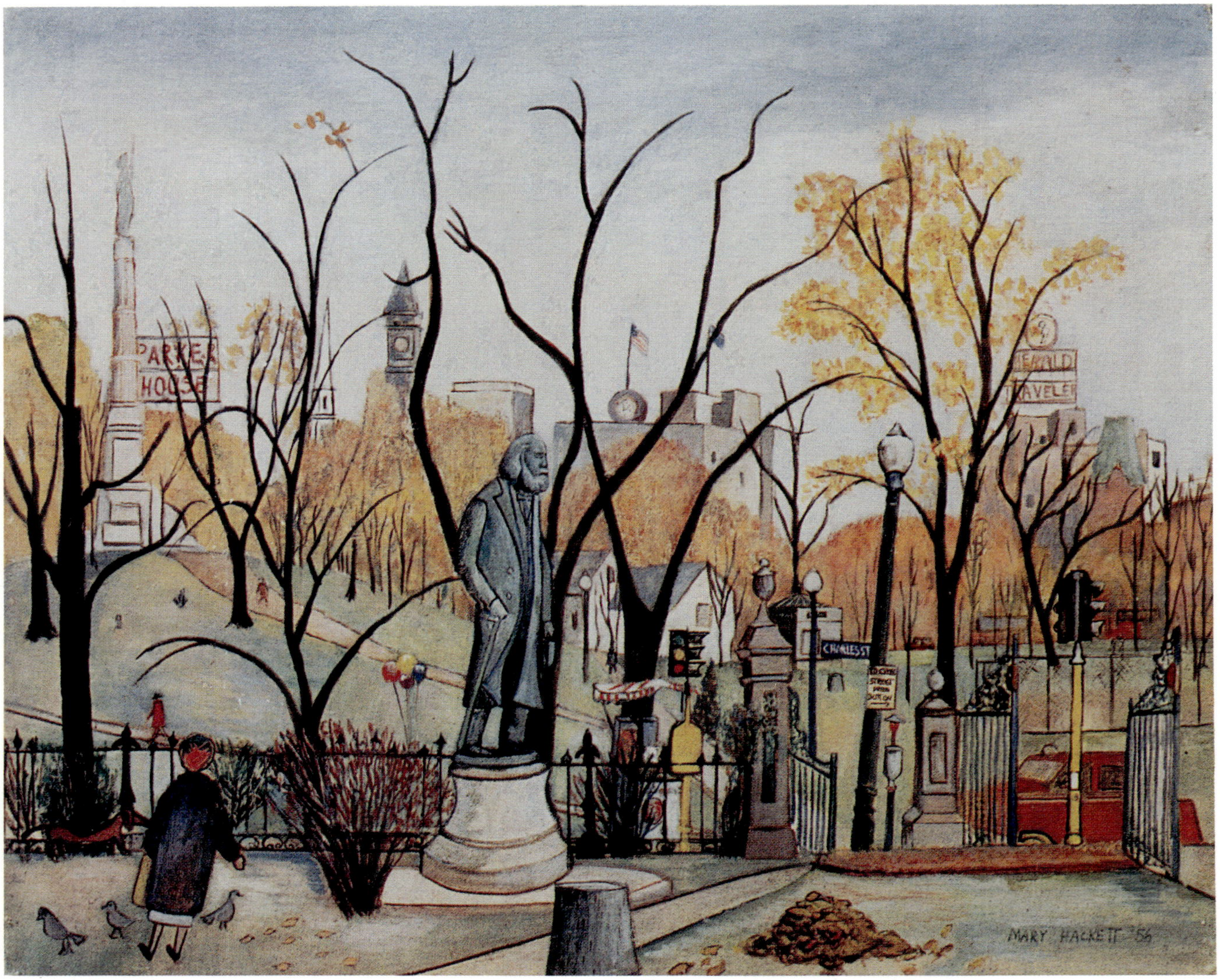

Statue of Edward Everett Hale (Boston Public Garden), 1956
Oil on canvas board
16 by 20 inches
Collection of John Dowd

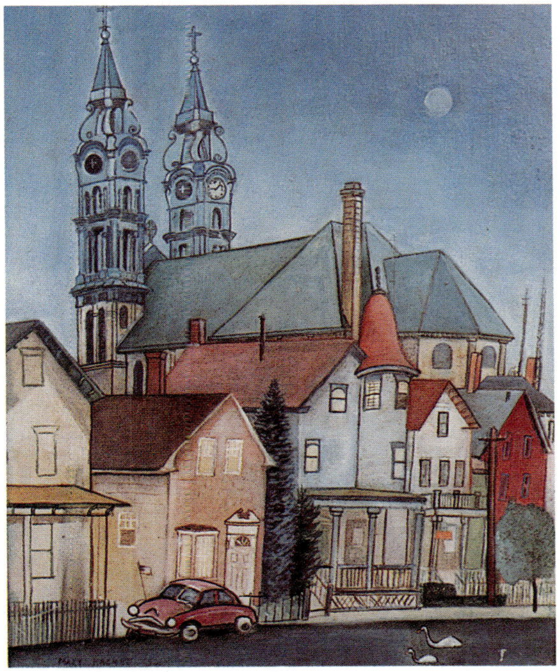

The Scary Cathedral of Fall River, u.d.
Oil on board, 24 x 20 inches
Collection of Tobias Everett

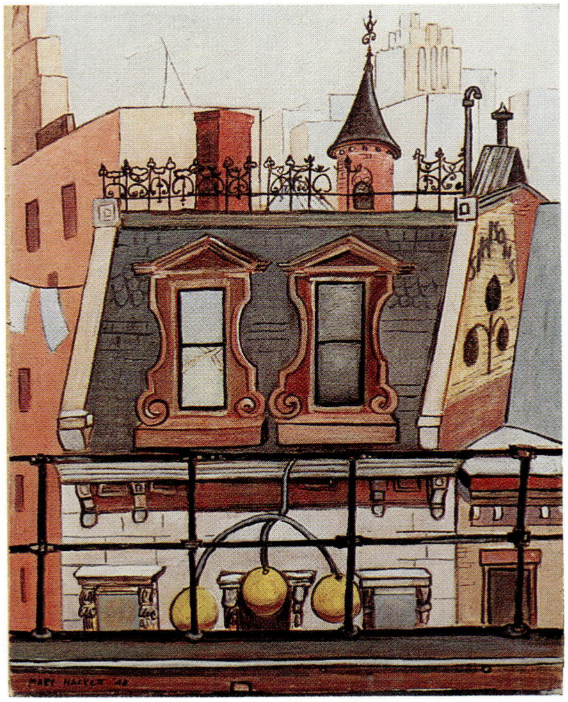

A Pawn Shop Viewed from the Old Third Avenue El., 1948
Oil on canvas board, 16 by 20 inches
Collection of John Dowd

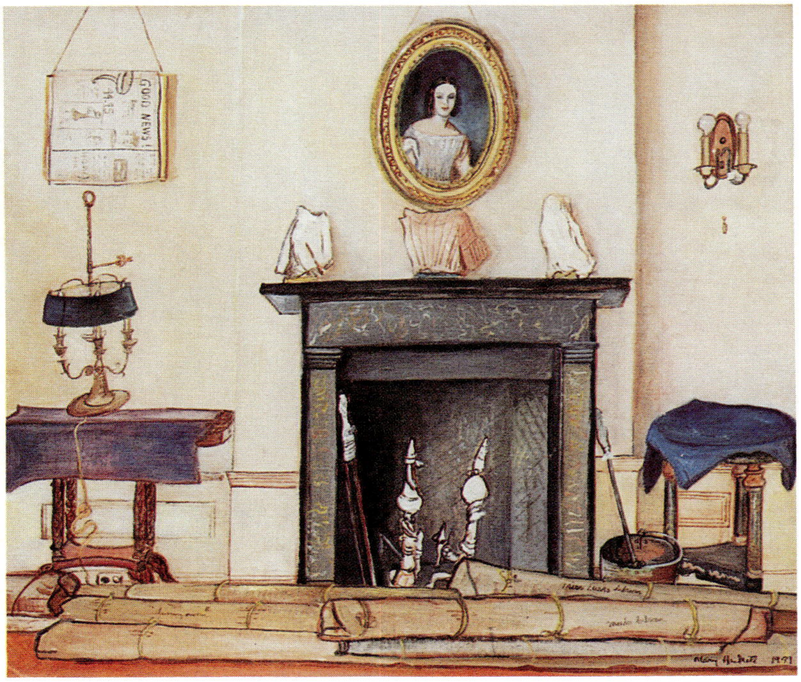

Aunt Annie's N.Y. Apt., 1947
Oil on board, 20 by 24 inches
Collection of Susan Baker

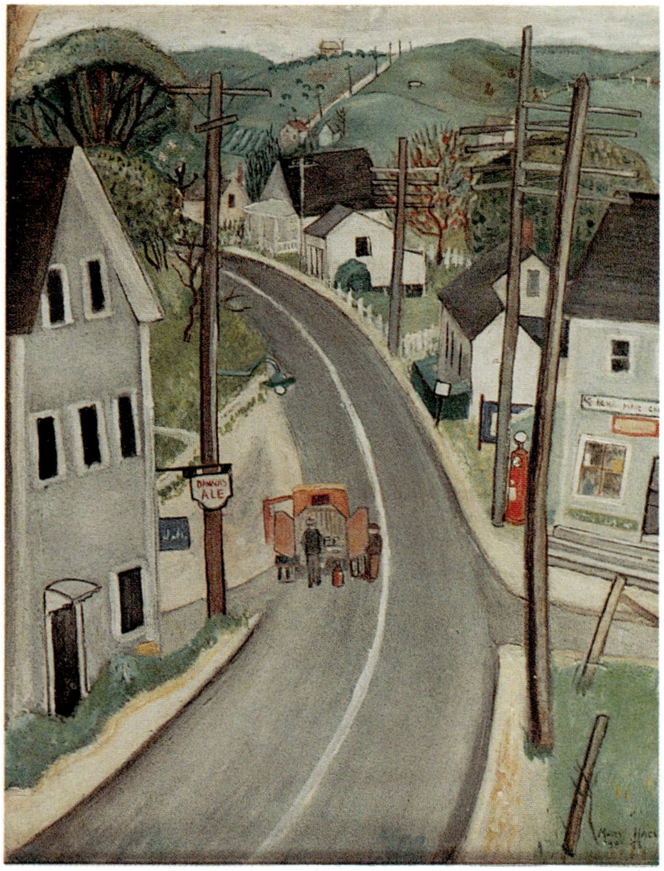

The Long Uphill Climb Ahead, 1938, 1943
Oil on board, 20 x 16 inches
Collection of Timothy Bright

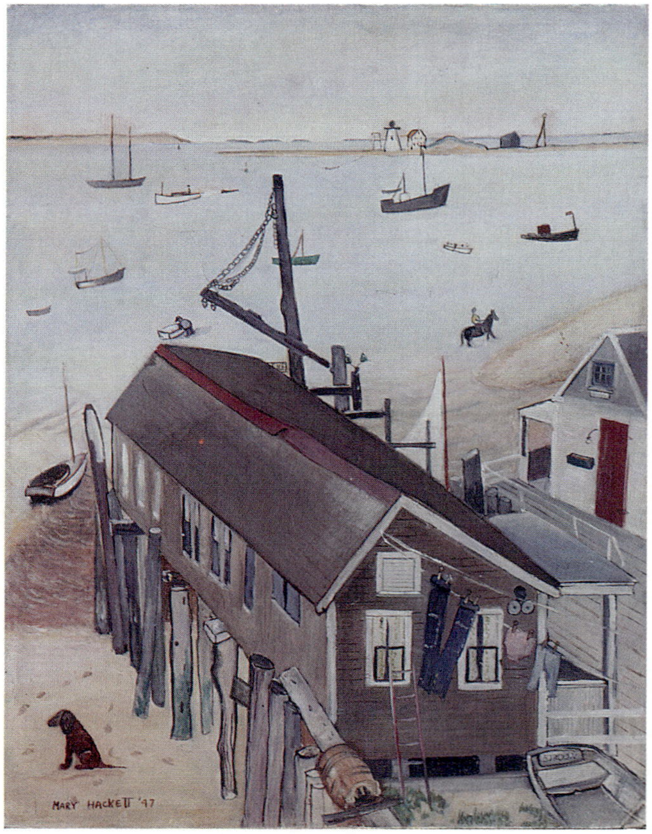

Low Tide, Provincetown (Horse and Dog), 1947
Oil on board, 20 x 16 inches
Collection of Blair Resika

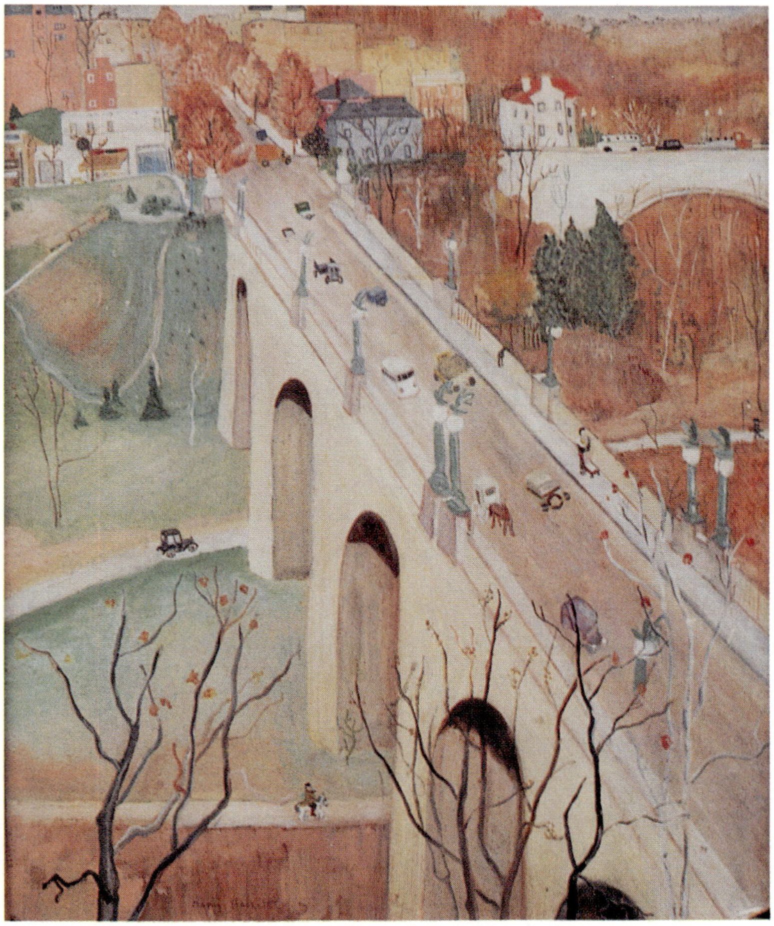

Connecticut Avenue Bridge, Washington, D.C., c. 1930s
Oil on canvas board, 30 by 25 inches
Collection of Mrs. H. Paul Althaus

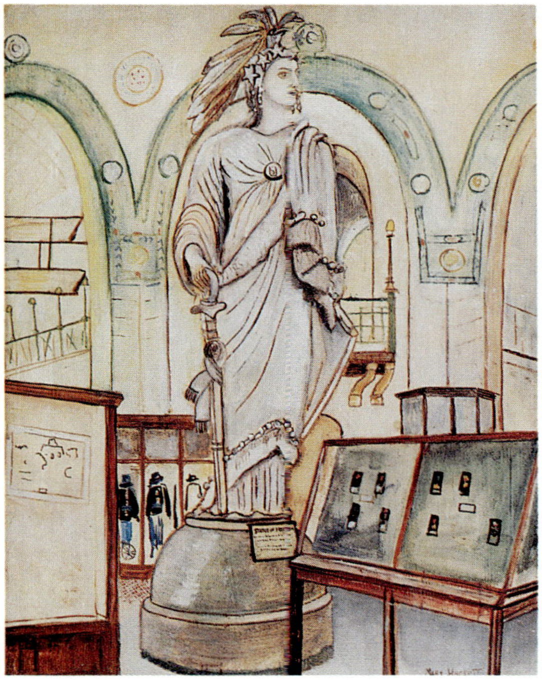

The Big Liberty Atop the Capitol, 1946
Oil on board, 20 by 16 inches
Collection of Susan Baker

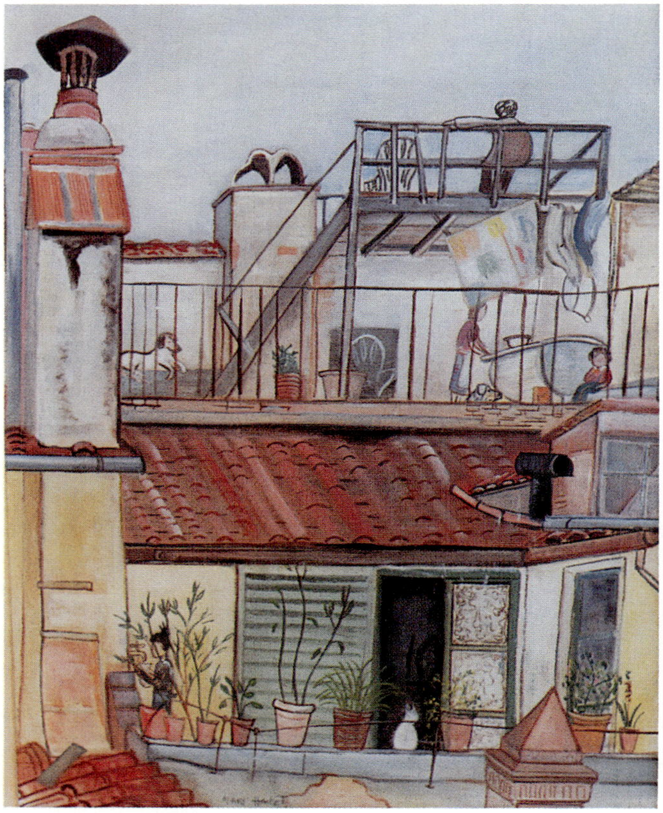

Pensione Bertolini, 1953
Oil on board, 16 x 20 inches
Collection of Wendy Everett

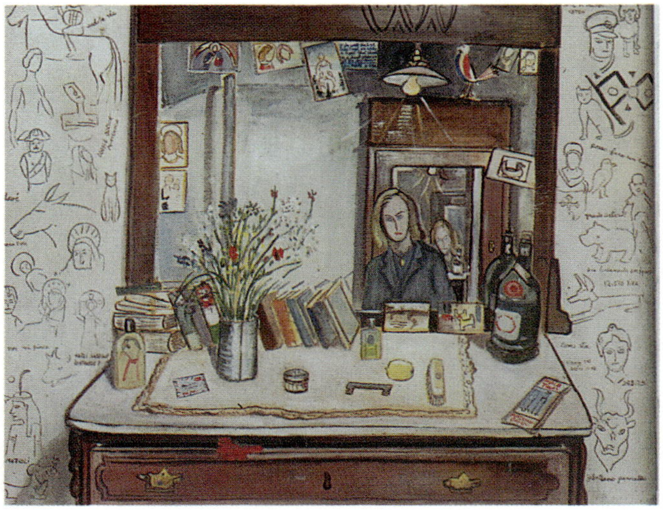

Pensione Bertolini, 1953
Oil on board, 16 by 20 inches
Collection of Susan Baker

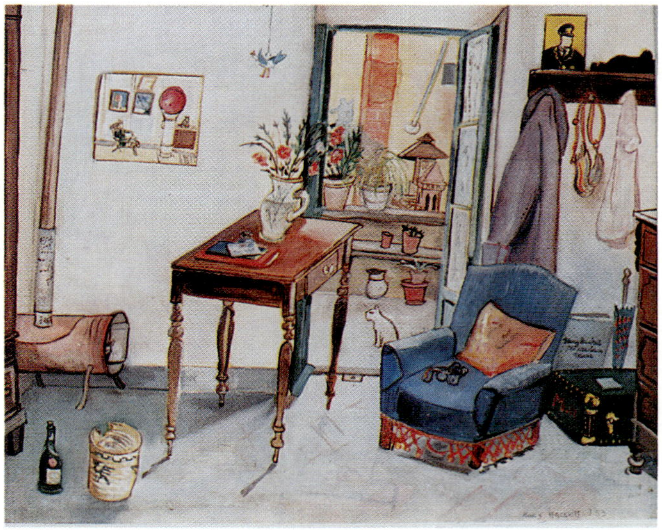

Pensione Bertolini, 1953
Oil on canvas board, 16 x 20 inches,
Collection of Susan Baker

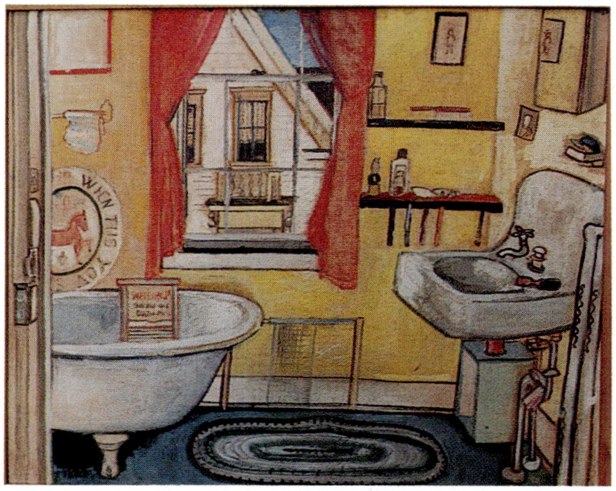

The Bathroom, 1953
Oil on canvas board, 16 by 20 inches
Collection of Frank Schaefer

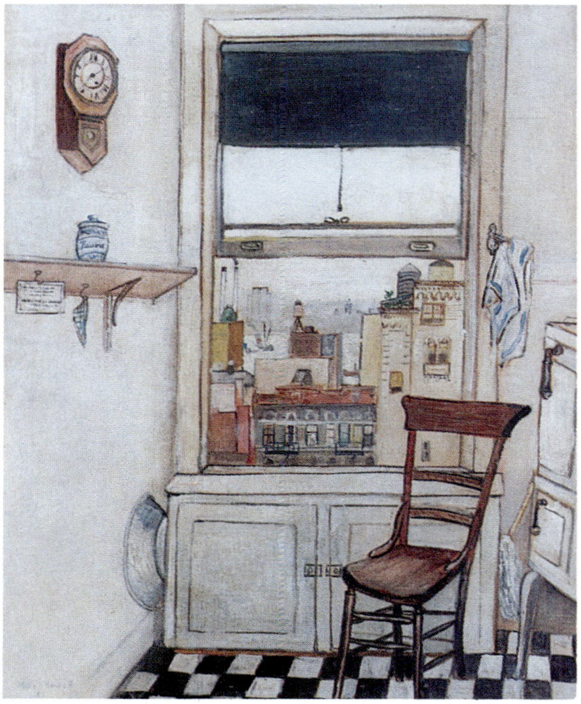

Kitchen, Aunt Annie's Apartment, 1948
Oil on canvas board, 24 by 20 inches
Collection of Wendy Everett

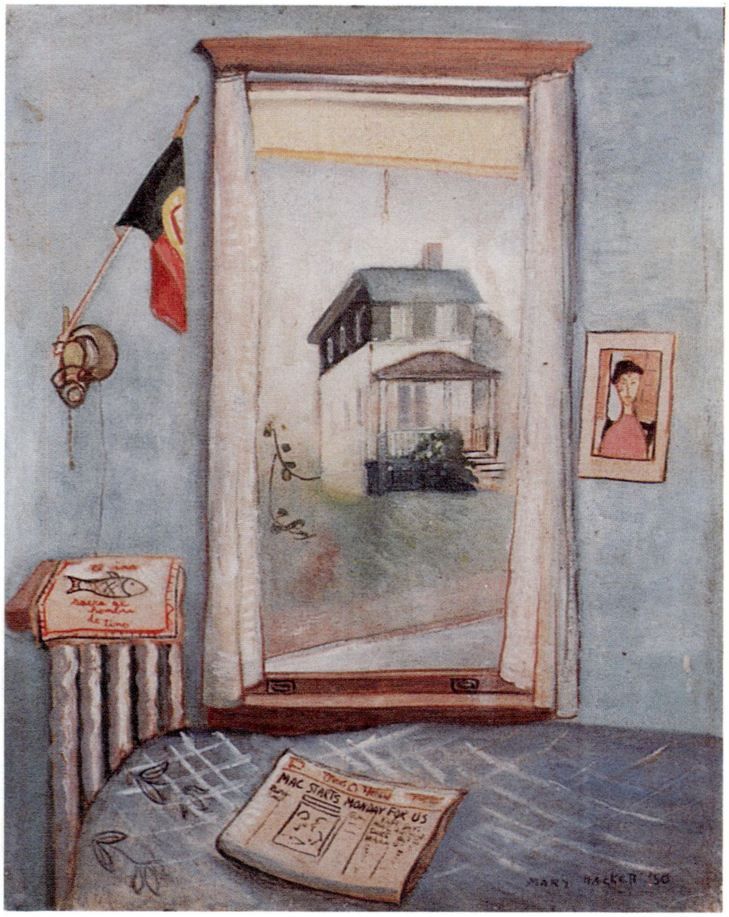

View from the Window, 1950
Oil on board, 20 x 16 inches
Collection of Tobias Everett

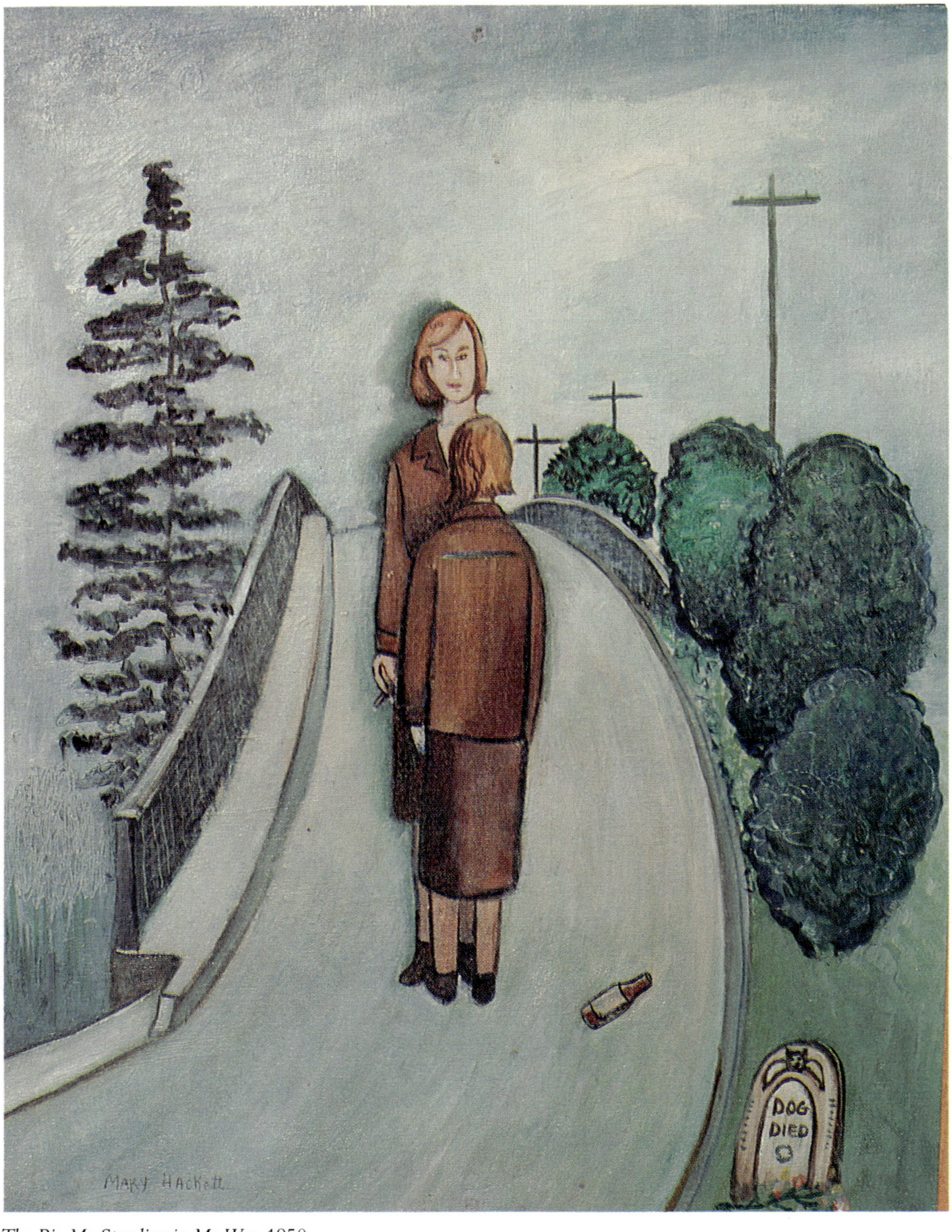

The Big Me Standing in My Way, 1950
Oil on canvas board, 20 by 16 inches
Collection of Jay Critchley

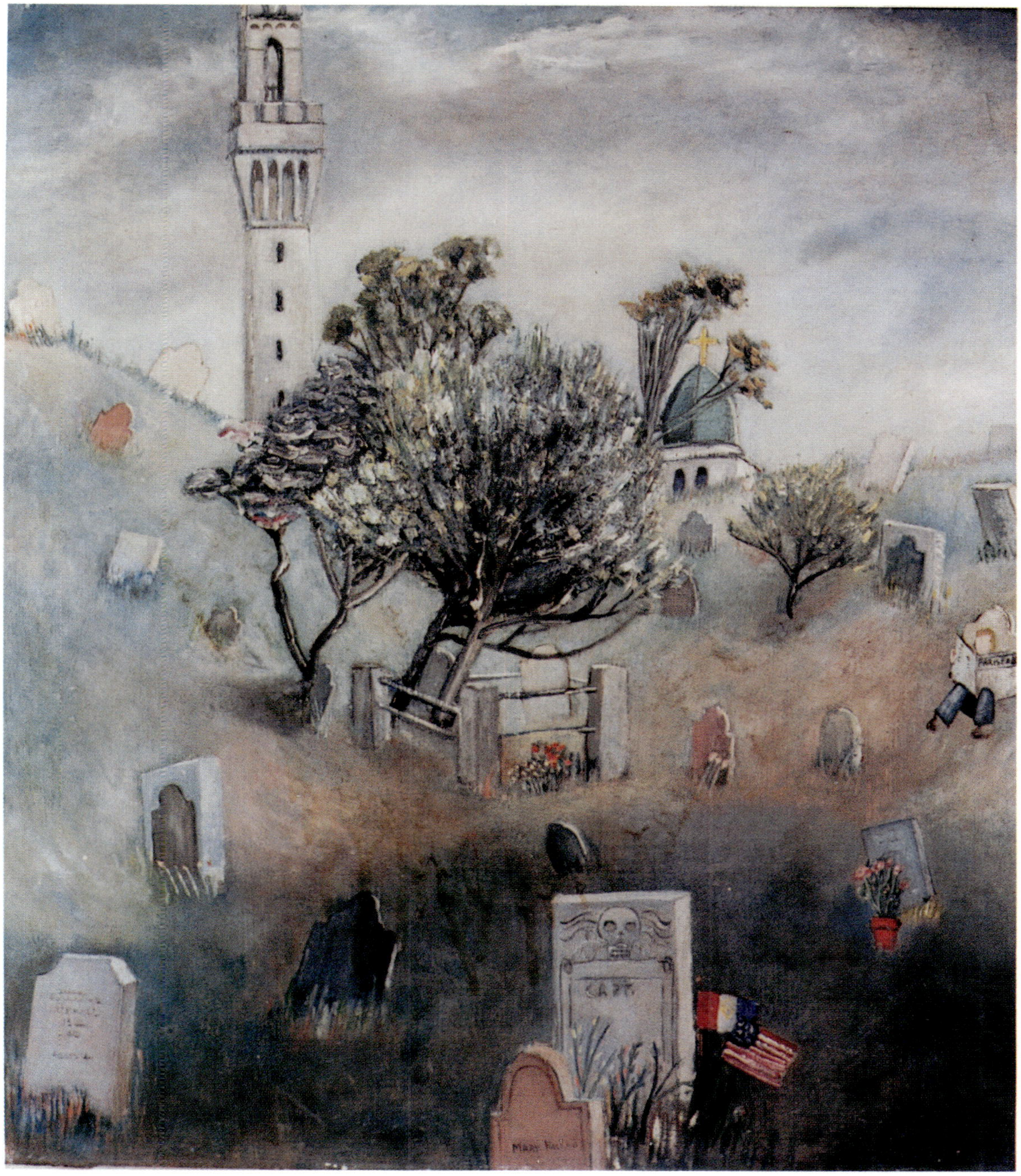

Nostalgia Over the News of the Fall of Paris,(Day in June), 1940
Oil on masonite, 20 by 18 inches
Collection of Saint Peter's Catholic Church

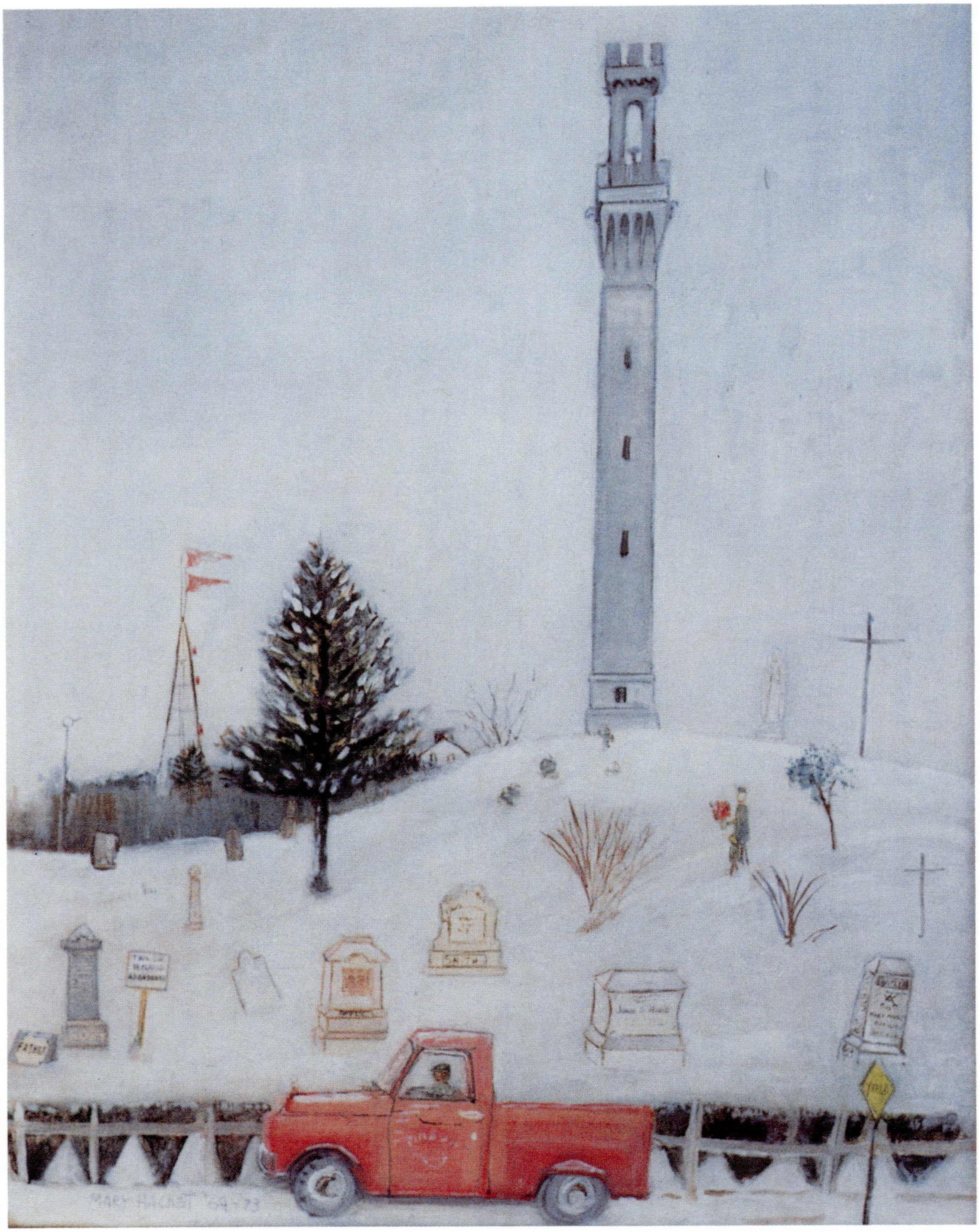

Provincetown Graveyard, 1969-1973
Oil on canvas board
20 by 16 inches
Collection of Wendy Everett

Three Reflections on Mary Hackett

1. On walking into Mary's (Bubs') kitchen we asked what that basketball-sized black spot on the floor was?? "I dropped a hot pan onthe floor and it burned the linoleum,--so-I just painted a big black circle there." Perfect.

2. Mary's interiors are special. I think it is because she was great at painting emptiness--- like walls, like the volume of a room.

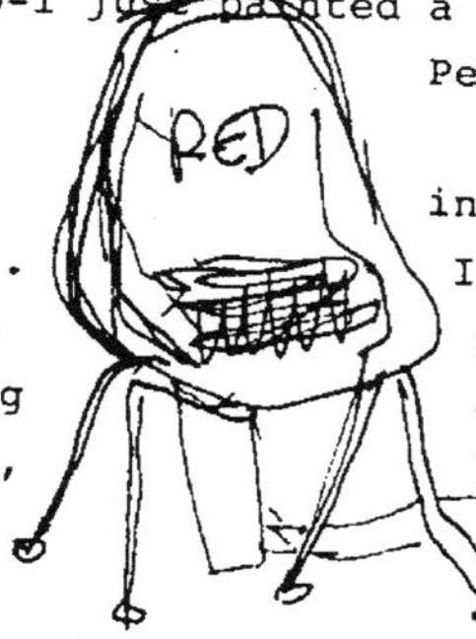

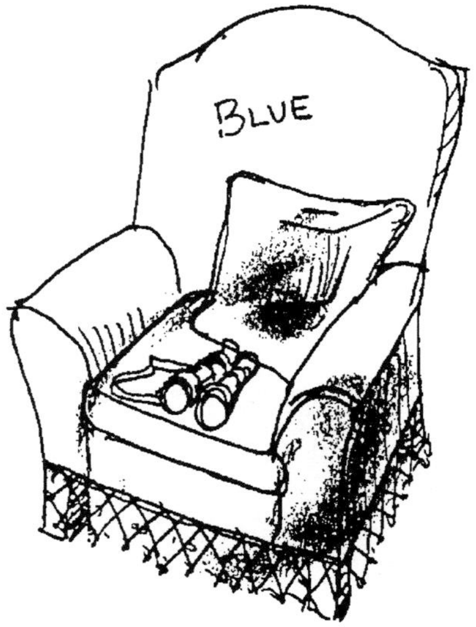

3. To me M.H.'s chairs were like figures or people in her paintings. I have sketched a few of these "friends" here ;-- a red FAWC chair at a Susan Baker opening,--- a moderne aqua job in front on an empty wall by a slightly ominous door, ---- a blue easy chair in a living room with pillow and binoculars(???) ----- and a blue/gray automobile seat seen from the back seat, complete with set of car keys. Vicky and I miss her.

Jim Peters

Vicky Tomayko

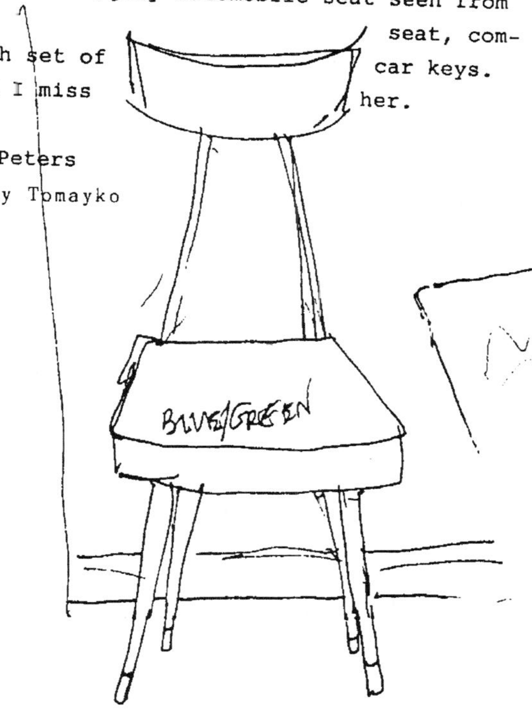

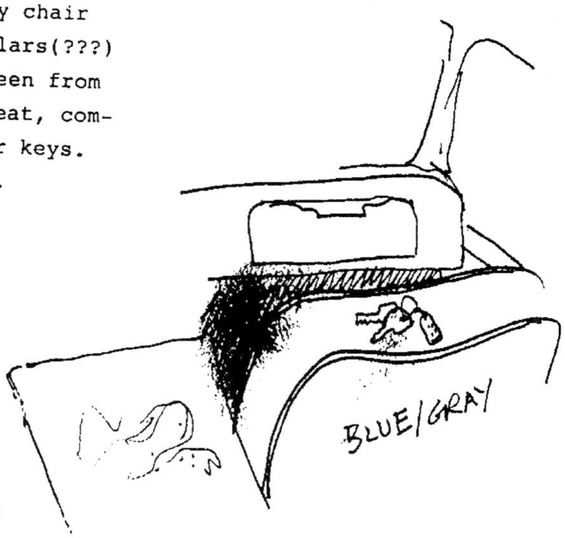

On Mary Hackett: Two Paintings and a Note

BY KEITH ALTHAUS

Open almost any book of "folk art" and you find an obligatory disclaimer about the inadequacy of the terminology and definitions of the field. We can dispense with that. "Self-taught," "eccentric," or whatever, Mary Hackett was a profoundly original artist. Her work, over half a century, will stand beside any. Though there is debate whether we should call the work of certain societies "art," either because they were not intended as such, or because there may not be such a designation within that culture, its power is undiminished. We can learn from that: better to look at the pictures.

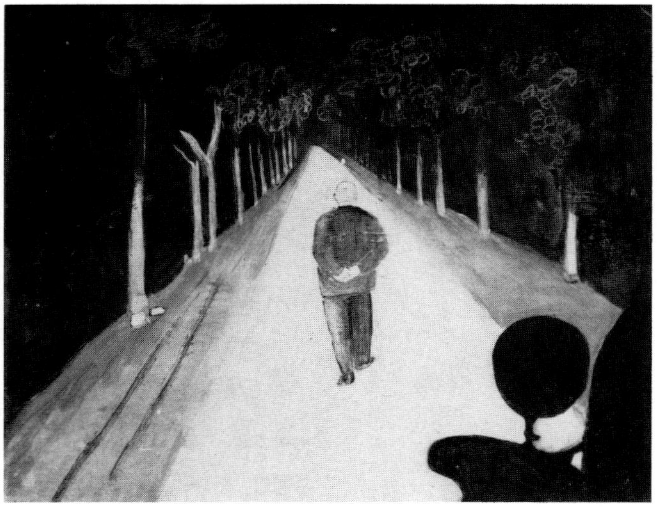

Khrushchev After He Got Bounced, 1973
Oil on canvas board, 8 by 10 inches
Collection of Susan Baker

"Khrushchev After He Got Bounced"

What draws me first into this inspired painting is the pathos, even humor, of the situation. But what holds me there is its powerful psychological atmosphere, unleashing several unnerving emotions not confined to the title drama. One is that peculiar sensation, due perhaps to association with search and interrogation, or with helplessness and the inherent danger and threat of being in the path of a car's headlights. A man in a suit in the woods at night is similarly disconcerting. One can't help but feel a suit is poor protection from the cold, and that however powerful our light, eventually the dark prevails. This little painting abounds with feelings of powerlessness and inevitability.

This picture is both unique and typical of Mary Hackett. Propelled by a scene, incident, or event, she casts it in its fullest implication, yet it remains in some way personal, nothing is inflated, there is no reaching. This "knowing" its place in the order of things is a kind of prescience not uncommon to the self-taught, the eccentric, or the visionary artist. While others seek discovery, or solutions to self-imposed questions, or even revelation in the painting process, these artists have no inclination to experiment but are concerned with faithfully recording, and with execution. On the backs of her paintings, where she often made pointed observations and revisionist commentary, she sometimes complained of her lack of skill but not her vision. In the beautiful painting of her husband reading in an armchair, he has no legs, because as she remarks on the back she "couldn't get them right." Those whose work is a composite of consciously chosen influences with a mandatory effort at newness can hardly compete for directness and natural power with those to whom an authentic vision has been granted. Those with a vision are charged with presentation rather than interpretation. Their truth is a given.

"Christmas on Bridge Street" 1939, St. Augustine

This painting is about joy. Inexplicable joy, that fills us for no reason. A balmy day outside the window, and you are alone in the house at Christmas. The dog has climbed onto the sofa, and then, as Yeats says:

> *My body of a sudden blazed;*
> *And twenty minutes more or less*
> *It seemed so great my happiness,*
> *That I was blessed and could bless.*

This is a secret the artist shares with us: while everyone was out I felt this. Peace, serenity, bliss: words from the vocabulary of religious experience describe it best, but it doesn't resemble that ecstasy of mystic revelation, more a messageless acceptance. Rather than a transporting it represents a returning, back to this body, this room, this afternoon, away from the distractions of desire and concern. Mary Hackett's paintings have always had a mild hallucinatory quality: her isolation of objects, clock, stove, typewriter, in a spare environment raises their status to that disassociative level Tennyson sought when he would stand in front of the mirror and repeat his name 50 times. Her wavering yet solid line sometimes seems not impossibly, the border of worlds; the austere, almost monastic walls heighten the effect. Her colors, neither gaudy nor jewel-like, have the harmony of another world: a minor chord, her haunting palette, resembling the colors of Indian corn.

There is an unquestioning quality about her work. We are spared "effort" and "effect." We feel everything she painted was important to her, at least in that moment. And because that obedience to what mattered, as opposed to fads and trends, guided her, most of her work "stands up" over 50 years. It convinces utterly and effortlessly. And with that saved effort we are able to expend our energy exploring and savoring the details, and the mysterious currents just below the surface. Her work is generally devoid of the qualities that distinguish the well-known "memory" painters of our time: sweetness and sentimentality. She shares with them a certain charm, an almost obsessive faithfulness to detail, an narrative directness and truth, and a lack of trickery and deception. She differs from them mainly in the complexity and the quality of her feelings This painting for instance does not pretend to resolve the numerous contradictions and tensions within it: loneliness contrasted wit the sociality of the season, the secular

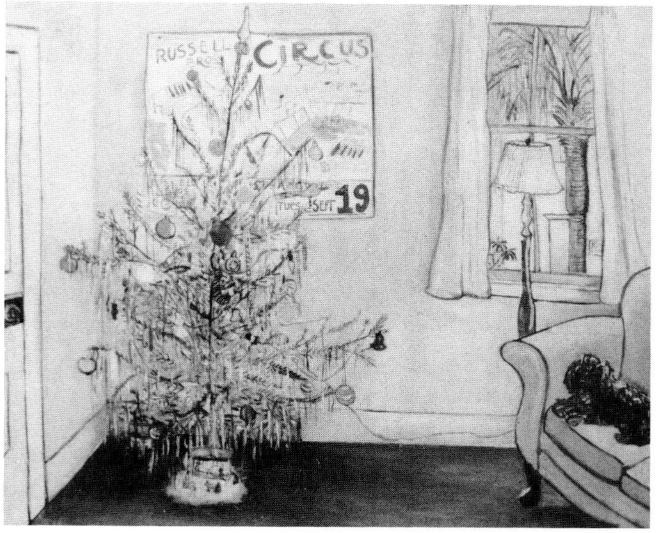

Christmas on Bridge Street, 1939
Oil on board
20 x 24 inches
Collection of Susan Baker

with the sacred, sparseness with clutter, interior with exterior worlds (even in this calm backwater one sensed the dark historical moment). But all are overridden, reduced to background noise, chatter down below, small and insignificant as voices in jars. A grand harmony drowns such "minor" discords. There is a place from which all things, even the most opposing, as Breton said, "cease to be perceived as contradictory." In such a place, often, and in many locations, Mary Hackett set her easel.

Note

I was moved by a photo in the local paper of her wonderful painting "Western School," 1941, whose faceless children led me to think about that recurrent image of emptiness and about her comfort with the absent. I have chosen to write about two paintings which represent ends of a wide spectrum. One is entirely imagined, prompted by the public announcement of the ousting of Soviet Premier Khrushchev. The other, the interior of a house in Florida, with her beloved dog Muffy Chargo on the sofa, comes from the artist's life. Disparate as they are, each is imbued with a special quality, one of the hallmarks of her work: they are at once intimate and mysterious. Although she worked in essentially the same style all her life, amid the ferment of the lively Provincetown art colony, she brought to her work a freshness and freedom, surpassing novelty, of conception and execution.

Mary Hackett was perhaps as singular and remarkable her person as in her art. And for many the two were inseparable. When I see her quiet "Angel in the Public Garden," or the gorgeous "Statue of E.E. Hale," exhibited briefly at the Provincetown Art Association last fall, I suppress a smile, remembering this was the woman who liked to paint statues because "they stand still." I fell in love with these painting years ago. Now if I fail to convince other of their beauty I will assume that the chemistry or the moment was wrong, and, because in a labor of love there is no tiredness, like a determined suitor I will try again.

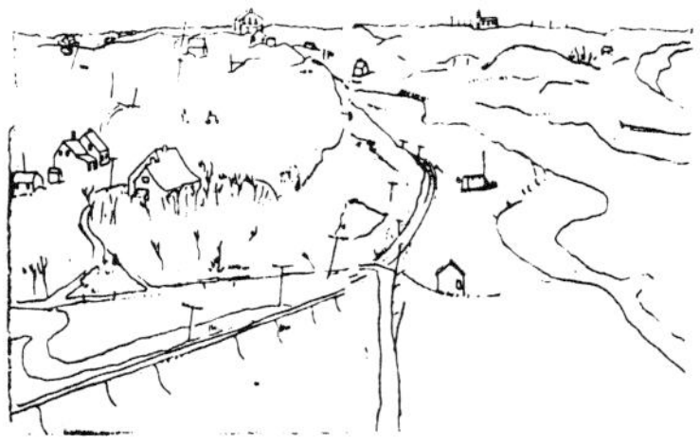

Corn Hill, 1945
Pencil on paper

Magic Mary Hackett

BY ROSALIND BAKER WILSON

When I wrote to Keith Althaus about his superb piece, "On Mary Hackett: Two Paintings and a Note," which appeared in *Provincetown Arts* in 1994, he suggested I write a little memoir. My place in Mary Hackett lore is that she gave me her very first painting. It was of her old-old-old-fashioned woodburning kitchen stove, which I lost. She reproached me for this on many occasions and on her death had her son, Thomas Truxtun Hackett, put through a call to me. She said she was dying of cancer and happy at the thought of dying, and reproached me again for losing her first painting. "I'm quite the thing now," she said. In spite of the reproach, it was an affectionate call.

She had forgiven me enough to give me another painting of hers, circa 1954, "Pensione in Florence." It depicts herself and a man at separate tables. Another client, a woman with a poodle, is reflected in a mirror over the fireplace. The writer, Dan Wakefield, upon seeing it in my apartment, said, "That's a novel."

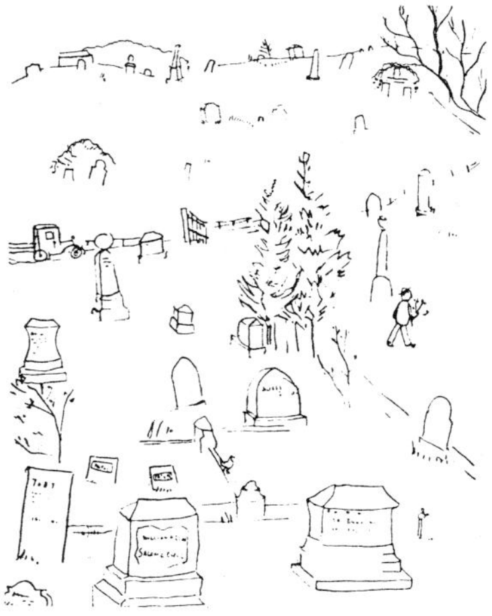

Provincetown Graveyard
Pencil on paper

Of the magical people surrounding my childhood and interwoven with my adult life, Mary (Bubs) and Chauncey Hackett were among the most captivating. Chauncey had been a law clerk to Justice Holmes, a successful Washington lawyer, married with two children. He had met Mary at a dance. They eloped when she was 18. He was some years older, with a brilliant mind, a rapier wit and more charm on the hoof than any man should have. Mary was tall, fair-skinned, with dazzling red hair. Over the years, each had tendresses for other people upon occasion, but they stayed together and produced enormously bright and attractive children.

A tendresse of Mary's was for Coulton Waugh and *tendresse* is le mot juste. Coulton Waugh, with a boyish manner, thick blond hair, and expert sailoring skills, was married to a very pretty woman, Elizabeth, a would-be painter, whose mother lived with the Frederick Waughs. Elizabeth had a fling with my father, who in true manner boasts of it in his diaries. Why didn't word get out? Don't sack up with Wilson—he kisses and tells. My best friend, Jeannie Clymers had another close friend, a beautiful Japanese girl, Tashi, who married Pete Seeger. Coulton played the guitar beautifully and sometimes alternated with Seeger at parties. Coulton's forte was sea chanteys—"When I was a little lad / My mother told me / You've got to hug and kiss the girls / Or you lips will grow moldy / Haul away, Joe, haul away." He was a romantic figure who turned the heads of myself and my girlhood friends. And gave Mary Hackett's head a spin or three.

Mary's father, Cleveland Moffet, was a high-profile journalist, writer of mysteries and children's stories, from Boonville, New York, five miles from where my father, Edmund Wilson, had his summer home in Talcottville, New York. He was some 30 years ahead of my father, had been editor of the *Paris Herald*, and also at one time of the *New York Sunday Tribune*. The pages which deal with him in the *Dictionary of American Biography* emphasize his fame for pointing out our unpreparedness for World War One.

I used to love to take my various beaux around to the Hacketts'. Very often Chauncey was there by himself, sitting at the far end of the sitting room at 5 Nickerson Street on a small Victorian sofa with a table with a chess board painted on it in front of him. The walls were filled with Mary's pictures, some of them cock-eyed, as Mary felt pictures shouldn't be hung straight. His favorite was a picture of some trains. He was a train man. He would send us out for ice cream cones or on occasion mix us some wondrous cocktail from outlandish combinations of juices and liquor. We would play chess and listen to his brilliant monologues. If he had a cold, he'd refer to *The Enormous Rheum*, a la E.E. Cummings' *Enormous Room*.

In later years, the age discrepancy changed the Hacketts' lives. He went into a retirement home, she converted to Catholicism and went into analysis. I used to kid Mary and say she'd converted too passionately, but her faith was totally sincere. She learned braille and taught it and always had some person from Catholic Charities she was helping.

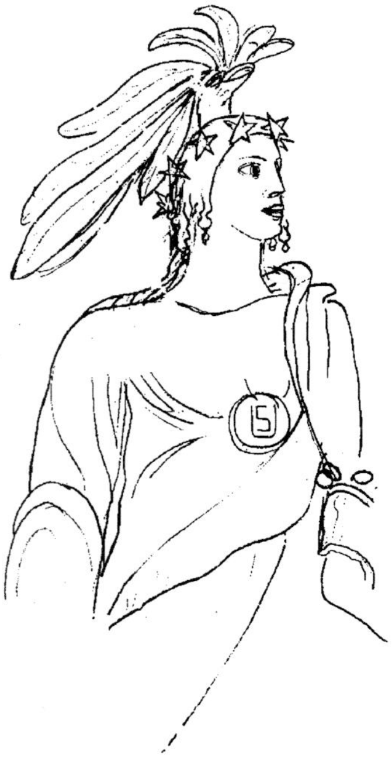

The Big Liberty Atop the Capitol
Pencil on paper

She eventually had an apartment in The Fenway Studios in Boston and commuted between there and Provincetown with side trips to Europe and the White Sisters of Mary in Saint Anne de Beaupre, where she stayed for long periods of time. She was bilingual in French and English. She gave them a white canary as she said that's what they looked like. After much soul searching, they accepted it as it was a communal canary, not a personal one.

An aunt gave her a minuscule island in the middle of a lake in Guilford, Connecticut, which she loved. She tripped to Boonville, her father's birthplace, where she discovered the enchanting little Catholic church and, Mr. Althaus says, painted some cows "in Edmund Wilson land."

Over the years any arrangements between the Hacketts and my father always resulted in confusion. In those days people occasionally went out on the fishing boats from North Truro with the fishermen to the traps early in the morning. You had to get up at two in the morning to breakfast and get out there. My father and I and the Hacketts and Chauncey's two elder children by his first marriage overslept or mis-met for a whole week before correlating ourselves and were wrecks as a result.

How did Mary's first picture disappear in my hands? She had painted the picture in a rented cottage on the West End of town, called "Way Up-Along" in the early '30s, while I watched her. I was 10 or 11. My best friend was Jeannie Clymer, daughter of the artist Floyd Clymer and granddaughter of the highly successful marine painter Frederick Waugh, who was also known as Wizard Waugh. The Wizard's paintings sold for enormous prices. Her uncle was Coulton Waugh, who did Dickie Dare and was later to become a successful painter. *Life* magazine did a piece, "Waugh *Fils* and *Pere*." The Frederick Waughs lived in what was to become Hans Hofmann's house, a house then full of Chippendale furniture and silver tea sets and a studio full of marine paintings. You felt as if the waves were going to roll in on you and fantastic pieces of driftwood, altered here and there so they represented people. The garden had plaques around it with pieces of sandwich glass he'd picked up at the old factory and inlaid. Coulton and his wife, Elizabeth, ran a hooked rug shop in the oldest house in Provincetown, almost next door, and lived in another house diagonally across Commercial Street from the parents. Floyd Clymer also lived in a house in a similar position to the Hacketts. The whole outfit was known far and wide as Waughsville as opposed to the East End of town occupied by the Dos Passos's, my father, who intermittently rented the house, and Susan Glaspell.

Until my early 20s, my second home was with the Waughs or Clymers, wherever they might be, with the result that I often left my things there or had them there. And the

Waughs and Clymers eventually moved to New York City after the Wizard's death and then to Newburgh, New York. Naturally, wherever they went there were canvases moving with them. I had the painting with me in my room all through Bennington but some time after that it disappeared amongst the Waugh-Waugh and Clymer canvases. Could Elizabeth Waugh perchance have purloined Mary's painting, as it was stored with the myriad other canvases?

Mary Hackett's "Pensione in Florence," exhibited at the Provincetown Art Association in 1954, has lasted well. I have looked at it sporadically while writing this, and there is something new every time The pictures in the pictures on the walls of the pensione, the dishes in the side cabinet, the flowers in the vases. It is a novel, as well as a painting, and brings back Mary, a woman of extraordinary innocence, humor and talent and fundamental reactions, never destroyed by the sophisticated milieu in which she lived.

Rosalind Baker Wilson is the author of Near the Magician: A Memoir of My Father, Edmund Wilson, *published by Grove Weidenfeld in 1989.*

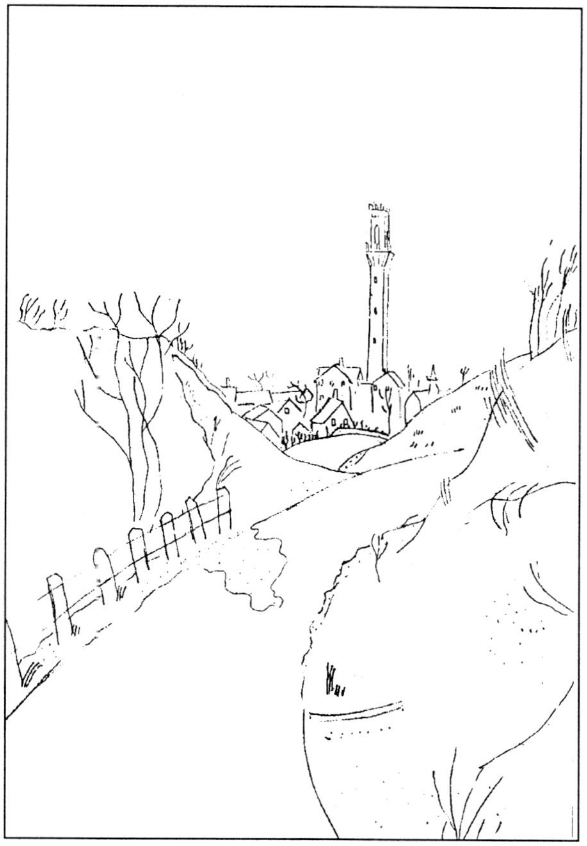

Pilgrim Monument, Provincetown
Pencil on paper

Further Notes on Mary Hackett

BY KEITH ALTHAUS

1

One reason Mary Hackett's paintings have the feel of "novels," as Rosalind Baker Wilson reports, is because they are full of suggestions and hints, plots and sub-plots, characters, and dramatic situations. In her landscapes a man walking a dog can assume great proportions and become a source of mystery or symbol of melancholy. Beyond this her works are novelistic because each is a full statement, made with extraordinary concentration and concision. They have an aura of completeness, wholeness, resolution. Here, we feel, is beginning, middle, and end. The are "big" in an unassuming way. They have a calm about them I am not sure the painter ever felt. But that peace is what she strove for. Camus' great line, "To create is to live twice," is subject to many interpretations. One implies that what we seek but cannot achieve in one life we may achieve in the other. For many art is an intellectual or emotional appendage, an added room in which to play or act out. But for others like Mary Hackett it is the same room in which they live transformed, or hopefully transfigured.

2

So many of Mary Hackett's greatest fans and collectors are fellow artists. She has a special appeal for them because they are in a position to recognize and appreciate the risks she took. Her boldness and sense of freedom exhilarate those daily faced with similar constraints and limits. In an age of great scale and deliberate shocks it is easy to overlook the fresh approach she continually exhibited in ostensibly conventional canvases. We are struck by her quirky content, her daring use of blank space, which can be as difficult and disconcerting as silence, the common touches that are so true they make you wonder why you only see them in her work. Where else have we seen so many dangling cords and electrical outlets! Often eccentricity and idiosyncracies lend credulity, since people assume, "It must be true because nobody would make that up!" In quiet but telling ways, and on a modest scale, much of the detail in her portraits and landscapes act to reinforce our impression of truth.

3

The growing interest in what lies beyond mainstream studio and academic art represent a hunger for authenticity and power. Our increased sophistication is measured by our knowledge of how we are being manipulated, by the our consciousness of the artist's intentions toward us. There is therefore special beauty and power in these works of a self-taught artist that were also to a large degree self-pleasing and whose motivation must remain a mystery to us. Their authenticity derives from their lack of self-consciousness. Their power is the gift of vision. Long after we have seen them, Mary Hackett's paintings resonate and occupy us. Stanley Kunitz says a good poem is one which never lets its energy leak out, no matter how many readings. Mary Hackett's paintings yield so much upon first "reading" it feels it will be forever before we've read all that is there. Even her most spare and simple canvases reverberate, reminding us how quickly combinations of a few numbers compound themselves, growing exponentially, approaching infinity.

4

It is always best to return to the work. In this case very little is readily available for public viewing. Today that is due to the fact that those who have her picture love living with them and are reluctant to part with them. Earlier I think she was under-appreciated. In the heated milieu of successive waves of art movements and their followers, she followed her own vision and was a perennial outsider. Working in Provincetown her work was essentially unchanged from her earliest paintings through her last ones, though Robyn Watson remarked that toward the end she used her oils almost like a wash, "as if she were running out of paint." In a less hierarchically rigid moment there comes time to consider her. Then, now, happily, after such neglect, we can invoke another sense of Camus' "To create is to live twice."

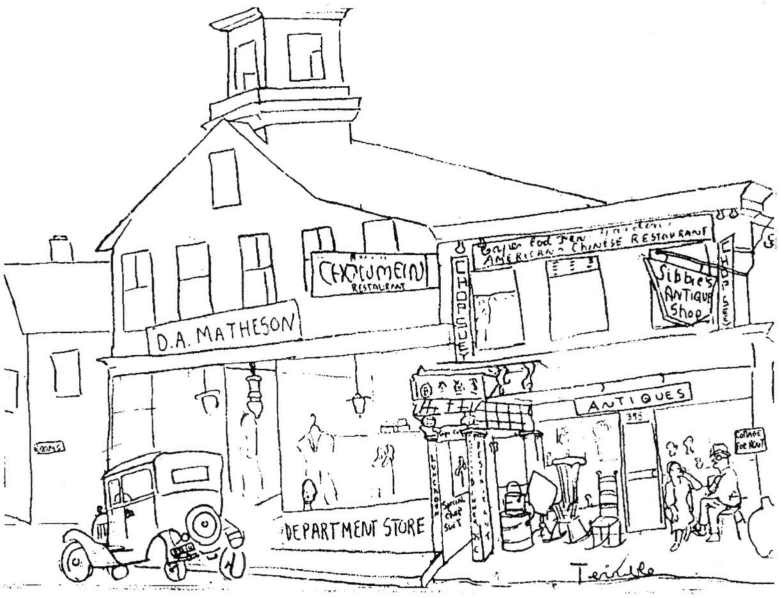

Provincetown Street Scene, pencil on paper

"Bubs or Mary"

An Interview with Mary Hackett, Provincetown, 1983

BY JAY CRITCHLEY

The following is an edited transcript of a radio interview with Mary Hackett, conducted by Jay Critchley for Provincetown radio station WOMR 92.1 FM in 1983, when Mary was 77. The granddaughter of an Episcopal minister and from a family of privilege, Mary Moffett Hackett wielded her way through a world which hovered between lightness and darkness. While her conversion to Roman Catholicism shocked her friends, it provided her with the fodder and the context for her peculiar slant on existence. Here was a religion which vividly spoke to her, which also reveled in the mysteries and paradoxes of life and the mythic battles between good and evil. While her paintings clearly included objects and rooms familiar to her world, they sometimes, when closely examined, revealed ethereal apparitions peering through windows, or faces erased or partly covered up. Her view of the world could as easily be seen through the window of her beloved car as from the waters of Provincetown Harbor, or eating lunch at her favorite no-fuss eatery, Dairyland, or through her vision of St. Ann and her daughter hovering in the sky over Provincetown, as depicted in oneof her paintings. And her view of Provincetown could only be considered schizophrenic: it was either "simply odious" on the one hand, or "simply delirious" on the other.

Jay Critchley: Today our guest is Mary Hackett, more lovingly know as Bubs to her friends. Before I met you I heard that you had critical feelings towards Provincetown, but now you've become a born-again Provincetown lover.

Mary Hackett: That's a good way of putting it. When I first came here in 1928, I thought this is the most wonderful place; this is where I want to live. We did move here, and it was only in the last 20 years or so when it got so terribly overcrowded that I began to hate it. This summer has been very very good for me. It has made a big difference in my feelings about Provincetown.

JC: What happened this summer?

MH: I changed my attitude. After all you can change your attitude. I began to stop being so gloomy, and always complaining about downtown, about how terrible it is, about that "meat rack," or whatever they call the benches in front of Town Hall. I'd bring a book and go to the bakery and sit on the meat rack and watch people go by. All of a sudden, I thought, this is a great place! You don't have to go to a show—there's a whole show going on right in front of you.

JC: You actually started hanging out on the meat rack this summer!

MH: I didn't do it as much as I would have liked to. Instead of crabbing about the corrupt politicians and how terrible the town is, all of a sudden I found that it's a funny place, a lively place, very cosmopolitan. You stay here and everybody that you've ever known comes back, sometimes too much so.

JC: Have you always felt that way about Provincetown?

MH: I've always had to get away from here in the summer. I mean sometimes in the middle of the night I'll get up and just leave, go to Boston. I used to have a studio in Boston to go to for 20 years. Or maybe just up the Cape. When we were really hard up, and could ill afford it, all of a sudden I'd have to go, usually to New Bedford, around that region.

JC: I don't think there are too many people from Provincetown who would want to visit New Bedford for a vacation.

MH: New Bedford was great—there were no tourists there. The minute I could get away from Provincetown, I would have remarkable recuperative faculties. The weight of the world would fall away from my shoulders. Then I could read, I could paint.

JC: You used to do paintings right out of your car.

MH: Always I've used the car to paint from. I have to sit on top of what I'm doing, and therefore I use the car.

JC: You actually see the car in a couple of your paintings.

MH: You can't do that all the time. One time in Washington I did a painting in the front of the White House and a lot of people would bother me while I was working. Then I stopped being disagreeable when they would come up and ask me things, and tell them that anybody can paint if you want to, that I just took it up in my 20s, that I didn't do anything as a child. I think one of the explanations of my paintings is that I never did anything at all as a child, nothing, and so when I did start to draw in my 20s, it was like a child starting to draw. Children's drawings are always good, until they get involved with older people that contaminate their influence. I think you have to start out by drawing. That was my method. The first thing I ever did was in Washington, an old canal by the B and O Railroad. I thought I wanted to write in those days. I went off with a notebook to write and I wasn't getting anywhere with the writing, and I just happened to notice this tree that had fallen over the canal, and I started to draw it. It was very mysterious.

JC: As a child no one ever said to you that you were an artist?

MH: Oh no! My sister was the artist! I was the worst one in the drawing class. So I attempted just a line drawing of this tree that had fallen over the canal. That started me off. And the minute I saw that I could do that, I was very, very excited. It was just marvelous! I would draw just anything, but it was mainly interiors — I had two small children at the time. I could see that the drawing was good, I recognized myself that these were good. It was extremely exciting. I was about 23 or 24. I didn't do anything but draw for three or four years, I was afraid of using any kind of color. I didn't want to, I didn't need to. I was happy just drawing, everything and anything.

JC: And you didn't have any classes or anything?

MH: Oh, no, that would be ruinous. That would spoil everything. Of course if you're going to be a professional artist, I imagine you need some kind of background of studying, but I would have been lost. My palette is a total mess, I just arrange the colors any old way. As far as the painting goes, that's one time that I really can't be told.

JC: So you feel fortunate you weren't ruined.

MH: I wouldn't have done anything, I wouldn't have gotten anywhere.

JC: Do you think that happens to many artists?

MH: I don't know. I think most artists think if they have talent, they should study. And they go to the Art Students League or something.

JC: You didn't think that?

MH: I wasn't in the position to do it. I didn't take myself seriously. I just thought this was fun. I didn't think of myself as being an artist at all. It was years before I even said that I was an artist. John Dos Passos, a friend of ours, was very systematic about working, Nothing interfered. He worked from nine to 12 everyday, holidays included, and then he'd have the rest of the day free. I asked him whether he got any pleasure out of his writing. and he looked at me askance, and he said "Pleasure! I've long since gotten out of the amateur stage." So you don't have pleasure unless you're an amateur, I mean I got that message. He said, no, it had gotten increasingly difficult, and you never were satisfied with what you'd done. And also Karl Knaths told me the same thing about painting. He used to walk by my house. I asked him whether he didn't get blocked. He used to also work very regularly. And he said, "Oh course I get blocked. I'm blocked half the time but that doesn't stop me from working every day." Well I never worked in that way. I had long periods when I couldn't work at all. And ordinarily I can only work if I'm in a good mood. Sometimes I've worked out of a very bad mood, and put it into the painting. But especially with my early paintings, it was all very happy.

JC: Have you had trouble in terms of people thinking of you as an amateur?

MH: Very few people really respond to my work at all. They don't think it's anything but an amateurish effort. There are people who like my work. They are very few. They tend to say, "She's a great genius!" That part I don't understand either. They build me up way beyond what I think it's worth. Very often my paintings have been rejected. They used to have a show in the Public Garden in Boston and I was rejected every single time—paintings that people now think quite a lot of.

JC: So your paintings really come from different places than those of other painters?

MH: I had to do it. I was really not too good as a housewife. With painting, I could get away. I never had a studio until long after my children had grown up, but I was constantly painting. You find the time. It's no excuse to say there's no time.

JC: So your work is highly personal and autobiographical in terms of your life and surroundings.

MH: In fact I think of my work as being like illustrations. I don't see what the difference is between my work and an illustration. "View of Nickerson Street" for instance—I'm trying to make a literal presentation of Nickerson Street, of looking down the street at Hans Hofmann putting out his trash. I'm trying to make it as accurate as I possibly can. I'm not trying to distort perspective. I've learned perspective the hard way. I haven't studied it, so I only know what I've learned, and it's all cockeyed, all wrong. But I'm trying to make it as literal as possible and it turns out totally different from the way it is. The street goes the wrong way.

JC: Does it turn out the way you want it to?

MH: I think it's just great the way it turns out! I like the way it turns out. The trouble with some of my more recent work is that it's gotten too literal, I know too much now about perspective. But now I want to be freer. I'm tired of this niggling way of working. I kept some old paintings, and I want to paint over them, using some of their underpinnings to show through. There's one painting I did when I was in a terrible state, a snow scene. The agony in that first painting was no good, but I painted something on top of it so the agony was underneath. That's part of life, you use the bad to make something better. And this can also apply to behavior.

JC: You've painted a lot of locomotives and steam engines. One painting has them standing on the track hissing and smoking but they not going anywhere.

MH: That was me, that was a self-portrait. Three steaming, hissing locomotives with no place to go! I mean these things come out, but I can't analyze it. The early ones are the ones I like the best. They contain the excitement of the beginning.

JC: Did you ever throw any paintings away?

MH: I'd tend not to because I'd keep thinking they could be used in some way by being painted over.

JC: Have you painted over a lot of paintings?

MH: Not too many, but that's what I'd really like to do.

JC: You mentioned seeing a psychiatrist and going to doctors. You were involved in therapy for a number of years.

MH: Probably my therapist is the more important person in my life. He was a Jewish convert to Catholicism, and he was the most fanatical Catholic that I have ever seen in my life—I being a convert myself from the Episcopal church. I was kicked out of the Episcopal Church, I've got to get that in! So I landed at the Catholic Church. He was a fantastic doctor. I went to him for several years beginning in 1957 and I've kept in touch ever since. It's almost 25 years now, and I still keep in touch with him.

JC: What was going on with your work at the time?

MH: I did a wonderful painting of his office. I'm leaning over in a bedraggled condition. He's standing in the door, the way he used to, looking sort of fat without any expression locked onto him. A priest is coming dancing out—he had a lot of priests and nuns as patients. He used to go to mass every single day at noon, and while he was away, I was making drawings in his office or waiting room. It was really an amusing painting that he hung up in his waiting room. In spite of all his holy business, he also admired my work very much and had a couple of other paintings hung up there. One day I got angry at something. I said you can have the paintings but I want the frames. It was a little rude of me, but you're supposed to say what's in your mind! He wouldn't let me have this particular one back for the show, and I would have really liked to have it. During the period with the analyst, a tremendously productive period, I was also writing poetry. I wouldn't be here now if it wasn't for him.

JC: Even for painting?

MH: For my whole life. He was a very intuitive man and very religious. He had a private line to God, a fantastic person.

JC: At the same time you converted to Catholicism..

MH: Well before I went to him I converted, but I found out I needed more than just the church. I needed therapy as well. I chose him. I was terribly opposed to any kind of therapy but I reached a point when I had to do something. The church wasn't enough. I wanted somebody who had some moral structure. I chose him because in the first place he was a convert and because he lived close to where I lived, on Commonwealth Avenue.

JC: Why paint? What's it for? Is it something that makes sense to you?

MH: I don't know. I can't answer your question. I can only say I feel fine when I'm working. It was a solution but it's not the only thing in the world. Why paint? Why write? Why live? I can't analyse it. I just talk off the top of my head. Everybody is several different people—I'm Bubs and I'm Mary, and I don't know which is which.

Jay Critchley is an artist who lives in Provincetown.

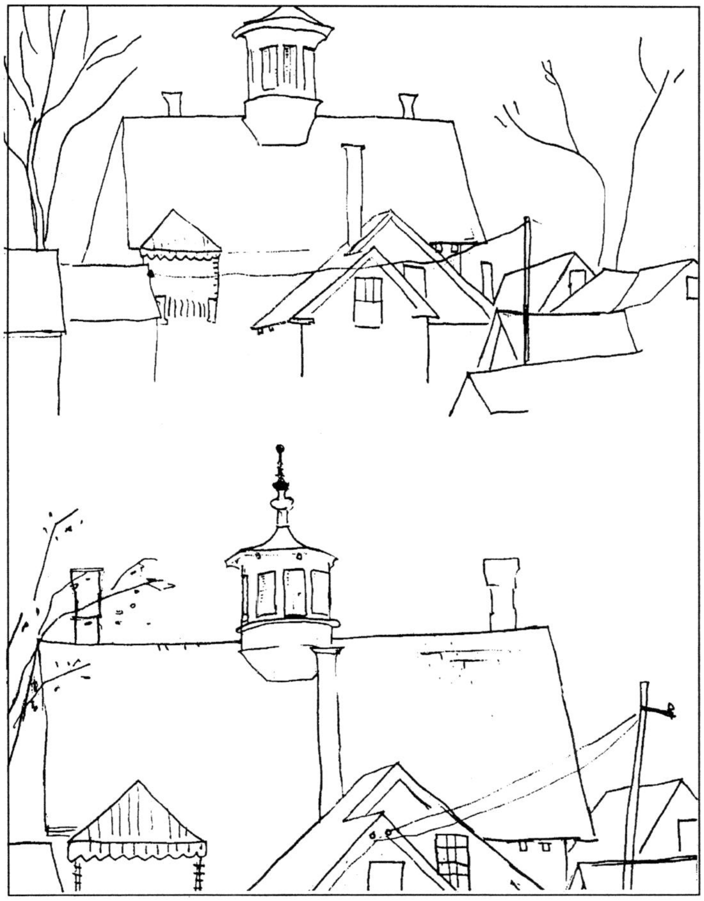

Provincetown Rooftops
Pencil on paper

Exhibition Checklist

Connecticut Avenue Bridge, Washington, D.C. (The Suicide), c.1935
Oil on canvas board
16 by 20 inches
Collection of Susan Baker

Dark Night of Clutter, (1923) c.1970s
Oil on board
20 by 16 inches
Collection of Ellery Althaus

Connecticut Avenue Bridge, Washington, D.C., c. 1930s
Oil on canvas board
30 by 25 inches
Collection of Mrs. H. Paul Althaus

The Hideous House on Thirtieth Street, c. 1930s
Oil on canvas board
20 by 24
Collection of Susan Baker

Connecticut Ave., D.C., c. 1930s
Oil on canvas board
16 by 20 inches
Collection of Rosamond Tirana

Untitled (Civil War Uniform from the Smithsonian), c. 1930s
Oil on canvas board
20 by 16 inches
Collection of Anna and Philip Hamburger

Paige's Garage, 1938
Oil on canvas board
20 by 24 inches
Collection of Susan Baker

Christmas on Bridge Street, 1939
Oil on board
20 x 24 inches
Collection of Susan Baker

Wendy's Room, 1940
Oil on canvas board
20 by 24 inches
Collection of Tobias Everett

Nostalgia Over the News of the Fall of Paris, (Day in June), 1940
Oil on masonite
20 by 18 inches
Collection of Saint Peter's Catholic Church

Untitled (St. Lucia Landscape), n.d.
Oil on canvas board
16 by 20 inches
Collection of Anna and Philip Hamburger

Untitled (Living Room), 1942
Oil on canvas board
20 by 24 inches
Collection of Diana Worthington

Andrew Jackson, 1943
Oil on canvas board
16 by 20 inches
Collection of Jack and Martha Hall

Portrait of Jack H. Hall, 1943
Oil on canvas board
20 by 16 inches
Collection of Noa Hall and John Williams

Darius, Leonora and Katrina Hall, c. 1943
Oil on canvas board
16 by 20 inches
Courtesy of Cherrystone Gallery

View of Corn Hill, 1945
Oil on canvas board
20 by 24 inches
Collection of Diana Worthington

Central Park, N.Y.C., 1945
Oil on canvas board
20 by 24 inches
Collection of Susan Baker

The Big Liberty Atop the Capitol, 1946
Oil on board
20 by 16 inches
Collection of Susan Baker

View Down Nickerson Street of Hans Hofmann Emptying His Trash, 1946
Oil on canvas board
20 by 24 inches
Collection of Wendy Everett

Coulton's Baby Chair, 1946
Oil on canvas board
20 by 16 inches
Collection of Anna and Philip Hamburger

Historical Museum, 1946
Oil on board
20 by 16 inches
Collection of Susan Baker

The Front Room, 1947
Oil on canvas board
20 by 24 inches
Collection of John Dowd

Guilford Clock, n.d.
Oil on canvas board
20 by 16 inches
Collection of John Dowd

Portrait of Martha Hall, 1947
Oil on canvas board
20 by 16 inches
Collection of Jack and Martha Hall

The Western School, 1947
Oil on masonite
20 by 16 inches
Collection of Gloria and Peter Watts

View of Provincetown Flats, 1947
Oil on canvas board, painted frame
20 by 16 inches
Collection of Blair Resika

Aunt Annie's Apartment in the Summer, 1947
Oil on canvas board
20 by 24 inches
Collection of Wendy Everett

Aunt Annie's N.Y. Apt., 1947
Oil on board
20 by 24 inches
Collection of Susan Baker

The Reflection in the Mirror, 1948
Oil on canvas board
20 by 16 inches
Collection of Wendy Everett

Kitchen, Aunt Annie's Apartment, 1948
Oil on canvas board
24 by 20 inches
Collection of Wendy Everett

The Silver Pitcher, 1948
Oil on canvas board
20 by 16 inches
Collection of Wendy Everett

Wood's Hole Train Station, 1948
Oil on canvas board
16 by 20 inches
Collection of Blair Resika

View from the Elevated (Third Avenue), 1948
Oil on canvas board
16 by 20 inches
Collection of John Dowd

Untitled (Interior of Mary Hackett's House), c. 1940s
Oil on canvas board
20 by 24 inches
Collection of Noa Hall and John Williams

Untitled (Graveyard), n.d.
Oil on canvas board with mixed media
20 by 24 inches
Collection of Rhoda Rossmoore

The Oldest House, c. late 1940s
Oil on canvas board
16 by 20 inches
Collection of John Dowd

Monroe Hall, c. 1940s
Oil on board
8 by 10 inches
Collection of Susan Baker

Portrait of Rudolf Hess, 1950
Oil on canvas board
10 by 8 inches
Collection of Frank Schaefer

Portrait of a Well-known Author and Son (Aldous Huxley), c. 1950
Oil on canvas board
10 by 8 inches
Collection of Gene Armstrong

House in Washington D.C., 1950
Oil on canvas board
20 by 16 inches
Collection of Erna Partoll

The Big Me Standing in My Way, 1950
Oil on canvas board
20 by 16 inches
Collection of Jay Critchley

Franciscan Monastery, Washington D.C., c. 1951
Oil on canvas board
16 by 20 inches
Collection of Gene Armstrong

Dreary Nyack Winter, 1952
Oil on canvas board
20 by 16 inches
Collection of Susan Baker

Deck of the Emma Bakke, 1953
Oil on canvas board,
16 by 20 inches
Collection of Susan Baker

The Bathroom, 1953
Oil on canvas board
16 by 20 inches
Collection of Frank Schaefer

Pensione Bertolini, 1953
Oil on board
16 by 20 inches
Collection of Susan Baker

Pensione Bertolini (Dresser), 1953
Oil on canvas board
16 by 20 inches
Collection of Susan Renehan

Hound of Heaven, 1955
Oil on canvas
15 3/4 by 19 1/2 inches
Collection of Susan Baker

Statue of Edward Everett Hale (Boston Public Garden), 1956
Oil on canvas board
16 by 20 inches
Collection of John Dowd

Untitled (Interior of Mary Hackett's House), 1957
Oil on canvas board
16 by 20 inches
Collection of Shirley Yater

The Angel in the Public Garden, 1958
Oil on canvas board
16 by 20 inches
Collection of Susan Baker

The Hatch Shell, c. late 1950s
Oil on canvas board
20 by 24 inches
Collection of Susan Baker

Doorway of 10 Rue Oudinot, Paris, 1961
Oil on canvas board
14 3/4 by 18 inches
Collection of Wendy Everett

View from Peugeot, Paris, 1961
Oil on wood
20 by 16 inches
Collection of Susan Baker

Fountain in the National Gallery, 1966
Oil on canvas board
20 by 24 inches
Collection of Mrs. H. Paul Althaus

Untitled (Ipswich Street Interior), c. 1966
Oil on canvas board
20 by 24 inches
Collection of Miriam Goodman

View Out Front Window, c. 1968
Oil on canvas board
20 by 24 inches
Collection of Reggie Cabral

Fall View from Back Truro Road, c. 1969
Oil on canvas board
20 by 24 inches
Collection of Reggie Cabral

Untitled (Nickerson Street Interior), c. 1950s
Oil on canvas board
20 by 24 inches
Collection of Miriam Goodman

Nixon Taking Oath of Office, January 20, 1973, 1960-1973
Oil on canvas board
20 by 24 inches
Private Collection

St. Anne de Beupré, c. 1960s
Oil on board
20 by 24 inches
Collection of Susan Baker

Provincetown Graveyard, 1969-1973
Oil on canvas board
20 by 16 inches
Collection of Wendy Everett

The Vietnam War, 1970
Oil on canvas board
20 by 16 inches
Collection of Frank Schaefer

Untitled (Front Room, Nickerson Street), 1972
Oil on canvas board
20 by 24 inches
Collection of Rhoda Rossm0ore

Abraham Lincoln, 1973
Oil on canvas board, mixed media
20 by 16 inches
Collection of John Dowd

Untitled (The Enemy Is Us), n.d.
Oil on canvas board with mixed media
20 by 16 inches
Collection of Rhoda Rossm0ore

Khrushchev After He Got Bounced, 1973
Oil on canvas board
8 by 10 inches
Collection of Susan Baker

Susan Baker's Show at the Fine Arts Work Center, 1975
Oil on canvas board
20 by 24
Collection of Susan Baker

Dog's Graves, 1978
Oil on canvas board
20 by 24 inches
Collection of Susan Baker

The Partly Opened Door, 1980
Oil on canvas board
20 by 16 inches
Collection of Susan Baker

Untitled (Ormond Hotel), 1985
Oil on canvas board
20 by 16 inches
Collection of Susan Baker

Untitled (Brick Town Flooded), n.d.
Oil on canvas board
16 by 20 inches
Collection of Susan Baker

Plaza Cigar Store, n.d.
Gouache on paper
14 by 18 inches
Collection of Wendy Everett

Untitled (Dressing Table), n.d.
Watercolor on paper
13 1/2 by 10 1/2 inches
Collection of Wendy Everett

Untitled
(Church Behind Wrought Iron Fence), n.d.
Gouache on paper
15 1/2 by 11 1/2 inches
Collection of Wendy Everett